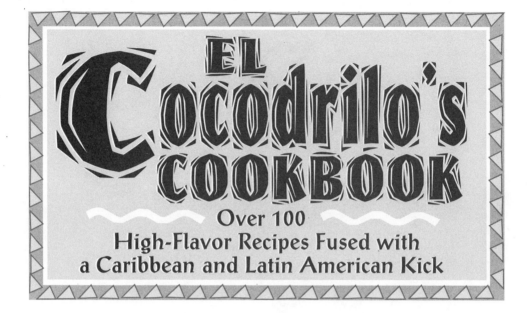

EL Cocodrilo's COOKBOOK

Over 100 High-Flavor Recipes Fused with a Caribbean and Latin American Kick

Marie Perucca–Ramírez and Julio J. Ramírez, C.E.C.

Featuring recipes by
Chefs Julio J. Ramírez, C.E.C., and Jefferson Seay
El Cocodrilo Rotisserie & Seafood Grill

Macmillan • USA

MACMILLAN
A Simon & Schuster Macmillan Company
1633 Broadway
New York, NY 10019-6785

Library of Congress Cataloging-in-Publication Data

Perucca-Ramírez, Marie.
El cocodrilo's cookbook: a celebration of the food from the
American tropics / by Marie Perucca-Ramírez and Julio J. Ramírez ;
featuring recipes by chefs Julio J. Ramírez and Jefferson Seay.
p.   cm.
Includes bibliographical references and index.
ISBN 0-02-861008-3 (alk. paper)
1. Cookery, Latin American.   2. Cookery, Caribbean.   3. Cocodrilo
Rotisserie & Seafood Grill.   I. Ramírez, Julio C.   II. Title.
TX716.A1P425   1996
641.598—DC20

Printed in the United States of America

10 9 8 7 6 5 4 3 2 1

Book design by Rachael McBrearty
Interior illustrations by Liz Cano-Manning

ACKNOWLEDGMENTS

heartfelt *thank you* to Linda Landucci for her wise counsel and insightful critique of the original manuscript; to Mary Josephine Morton Cain for her moral support in making this labor of love a reality; to sous chef Yonis Majano for developing and perfecting some of our wonderful desserts; to chef Aaron Aronson for his culinary genius and inspired recipes; to the kitchen staff at El Cocodrilo for the culinary alchemy they perform daily, transforming the gifts of the earth into gifts for the table; to our editor, Emily Nolan, for her patient and persistent efforts to keep the multifaceted book on track; and to everyone involved in this project for their belief in and commitment to the philosophy and goals of El Cocodrilo.

MP-R & JJR

A special *thank you* to Marie Magadaleno for assuming many of my restaurant responsibilities so that I could focus on the research and writing of this book.

MP-R

CONTENTS

About El Cocodrilo
Rotisserie & Seafood Grill

ollowing the success of their award-winning Fishwife Seafood Restaurants, partners Julio J. Ramírez, Marie Perucca-Ramírez, and Jefferson Seay wanted to open another restaurant with a similar focus—fresh, flavorful, healthful cuisine, skillfully prepared and offered at reasonable prices—but with a more global view. Drawing on the foods of Julio's childhood in Nicaragua and the talents of their kitchen crew, the partners created a Latin fusion cuisine which combined the spirit and flavor of tropical America with California technique and style. The resulting restaurant, El Cocodrilo Rotisserie & Seafood Grill in Pacific Grove, California, received rave reviews at the opening in October of 1990. The atmosphere at El Cocodrilo (the Crocodile) is casual and fun; the restaurant is decorated with masks, pottery, weavings, animal sculptures, and photographs of the American tropics, and it features a vibrant rainforest mural.

While El Cocodrilo supports local community projects and fund-raisers, its special cause is the rain forest and, in particular, the Orinoco crocodile. In honor of the crocodile, the restaurant's namesake, El Cocodrilo donates a percentage of its gross sales to the Orinoco Crocodile Project in Venezuela. Sponsored by the Wildlife Conservation Society (founded in 1895 as the New York Zoological Society), the Orinoco Project has established a biological research station in the newly created Santos Lusardo National Park, and is breeding and releasing captive-reared Orinoco crocodiles into the Capanaparo River in an attempt to save the species from extinction.

El Cocodrilo also features many dishes on its menu made with Brazil nuts and cashews. These nuts are cash crops for many traditional cultures living in the Amazon Basin. By using these foods in its cuisine, El Cocodrilo is helping to support the economic bases of these native peoples and in turn preserve the rain forest.

FOREWORD

his cookbook is a collection of those recipes we use at El Cocodrilo, a celebration of the food of the American tropics: Central and South America, and the Caribbean. We put special emphasis on food items that originated here in the Western Hemisphere. This book, as well as the cuisine we serve, is dedicated to the rain forest and its many denizens—that unique biosphere that gave rise to, and continues to sustain, the traditional cultures of tropical America. Interspersed throughout this cookbook are mini-profiles of some of the creatures of the American rain forest, recognizing their important contribution to the equilibrium of their delicate environment. We are increasingly hopeful that as our generation comes to appreciate and value this vast, yet fragile, green wilderness, we will be able to work together productively to protect the remaining rain forest from our own selfish interests. Knowing how interdependent we are with all other living species on this earth, we must strive to preserve and renew this living treasure for our children and the children who follow them. The preservation of the rain forest's ecosystem could well be our generation's greatest contribution to the future of our planet.

RAMPHASTOS SULFURATUS

INTRODUCTION

The sixteenth century marked the beginning of a great food exchange between two worlds. Over the millennia, civilizations thriving in both the Eastern and Western Hemispheres had developed distinctive agricultural inventories and culinary styles. Divided by great oceans, each hemisphere was arguably unaware of the other's existence. When Europeans sailed to the lands in the west, these ocean barriers were breached and the civilizations of Europe, Asia, and Africa met those of North, Central, and South America. This multicultural encounter resulted in an exchange of foods and cooking techniques, enriching the cuisine of peoples on both sides of the world.

The Europeans originally had gone to the Americas with plans to conquer and colonize the lands and to convert the native populations to the Christian religion. They sought gold, land, power, and religious dominance; however, it was actually the humble plant seeds and cuttings they sent back to the Old World more than the shiploads of gold and silver that proved to be the real treasures of the Americas. These foods, distributed by trade and travel to the far corners of the earth, became staples and cash crops for many peoples, enriching the diet of the entire planet.

With the dispersal of the food of the Americas throughout the world, the foreign cultures accepted, adapted, and then adopted these new foods as their own. The habitual use of certain key ingredients, flavorings, and cooking methods is what allows us to identify these cuisines by name, using such simple terms as *Chinese* and *Mexican*. For members of each ethnic group, the flavors and aromas of their traditional cuisine evoke memories of home. Though many of us are unaware of it, the sixteenth-century meeting of the Eastern and Western Hemispheres had a profound impact on many of these ethnic cuisines. Most people would be surprised to know that some of the key ingredients in the "traditional" cuisines of Europe, Africa, and Asia had come from the Americas only a few hundred years ago: the chiles in Szechwan and Thai cooking, the corn in Zimbabwean sadza, the tomatoes in Italian pasta sauces, the peanuts in Indian curries, the potatoes in Russian vodka, and the chocolate in Swiss confectionery are a few examples.

Since the sixteenth century and transoceanic travel, many food boundaries have been broken: trade, migration, and even war have carried the seeds of the world's agricultural larder to the farthest-flung cultures on earth. Chiles grow in Thailand, sweet potatoes in China, prickly pears in South Africa, pineapples in Malaysia, peanuts and cocoa in Sudan, potatoes in Nepal, and corn in Italy. Each of the cultures has adopted these new ingredients and made them its own. So the cuisine we identify today as Italian or Indian, Mexican or Moroccan is actually in great part the outcome of the transoceanic food exchange that began with the European quest for colonies and trade routes, a quest that resulted in the discovery and dissemination of the greatest bounty of the Americas: food. And while the dissemination went both ways—items such as dairy products, wheat, sugar, and rice were introduced into the cuisine of the New World—this book will focus on those foods which originated here in the Americas and went on to transform the cuisines of other countries around the world.

THE HISTORY OF THE BOUNTY OF THE AMERICAS

Imagine . . .

When the Spanish conquistadors marched into the Aztec capital of Tenochtitlán in 1519, they were unprepared for the splendor and sophistication of this metropolis. Tenochtitlán, the religious and administrative center of a powerful empire, covered ten square miles and supported a population of perhaps three hundred thousand—several times larger than sixteenth-century London.

Imagine Tenochtitlán as seen through the eyes of an Old World traveler who is entering the city the first time . . .

> . . . a city of tall stone temples, elaborate ceremonial buildings, palaces, schools, orchards, and gardens.
>
> . . . a city with wide, spacious roadways; canals; drawbridges; and aqueducts.
>
> . . . a city at the center of trade routes, which radiate hundreds, even thousands, of miles throughout the Aztec Empire and beyond.
>
> . . . a city visited by trade caravans, traveling by foot and carrying the goods of two continents over these far-flung routes.

Now imagine an immense open marketplace full of people, movement, and color. The marketplace is divided into sectors, depending on the wares of the merchants....

> ... sectors for goldsmiths and silversmiths, who offer exquisitely crafted jewelry and tableware.

> ... sectors for feather workers, who fashion the brilliant plumes of quetzals and macaws into capes, shields, headdresses, and ceremonial fans.

> ... sectors for fruit, vegetable, and condiment sellers.

> ... sectors for fishmongers and butchers, who display dressed fish, venison, rabbit, wild duck, and peccary as well as live turkeys, dogs, iguanas, armadillos, and turtles.

> ... sectors for people who sell flowers and ornamental plants.

> ... sectors for weavers of fine cotton and other cloth as well as for leather workers.

> ... sectors for potters, ceramists, and copperworkers.

> ... sectors for medicine sellers, who offer more than one thousand medicinal and magical plants that cure disease, induce hallucinations, and cast and ward off spells.

> ... sectors for those who sell cosmetics.

> ... sectors for rope and cord makers and thread spinners.

> ... sectors for those who sell pets, including birds and monkeys.

> ... sectors for specialty items where, in one particularly popular stall, a man sells syrup-sweetened snow brought down from the peaks of a volcano.

Smell the tantalizing aromas wafting from the food vendors' stalls ... the delicious scents of corn tortillas roasting on clay comals, herb- and pepper-spiced stews thickened with seeds or nuts simmering on open fires, steaming tamales, and barbarcoa from smoking stone-lined earthen pits....

Now stroll through the stalls of the fruit and vegetable merchants.... Marvel at the multicolored baskets overflowing with papayas, chiles, pineapples, guavas, peanuts, vanilla beans, corn, pumpkins, plums, avocados, squash, beans, potatoes, sunflower seeds, pine nuts, cactus fruit, tomatoes, tapioca, and cocoa....

...the bounty of the Americas.

This was the New World that the Europeans entered with their voyages of discovery, beginning in the late fifteenth century. The uniquely rich and nourishing array of fruits and vegetables on display at the marketplace at Tenochtitlán represented the culmination of thousands of years of cultivation and development by New World agriculturists. The arrival of the Europeans would throw this world into social, political, and cultural chaos, for the Europeans had come to plunder, conquer, and convert. While the thrones of Europe fought to fill their coffers with gold and silver, the real treasure of the Americas—her agricultural storehouse—was being dispersed in the form of seeds to the far corners of the earth. Through trade and migration, the seeds of the Americas were carried across the oceans to the savannas of Africa, the high desert of China, the steppes of Russia, the valleys of Europe, enriching all the peoples of the world.

A BRIEF HISTORY OF AGRICULTURE IN THE NEW WORLD

The agricultural bounty displayed in the marketplace at Tenochtitlán in 1519 was the product of two continents, many cultures, and thousands of years of careful sorting and tending of seeds. There were two primary centers of agricultural innovation in the New World: south-central Mexico and the Yucatán Peninsula; and the Andes Mountains of Peru and Ecuador.

Around eight thousand years ago in Mexico, Meso-American peoples developed methods of primitive farming. These early agriculturists were able to supplement their diet of wild plants and animals with plants that they cultivated themselves. Evidence found in caves in Tamaulipas, Mexico, shows that between seven and five thousand years ago, early Americans had begun to domesticate summer squash and grow chile peppers for seasonings. Bottle gourds provided both food and material goods: The fruit was eaten when it was young and tender, and the mature, hard-shelled gourds were hollowed out and used as water containers. The grain amaranth was also cultivated by the early Meso-Americans. The domestication of corn,

El Cocodrilo's Cookbook

around 2500 B.C., was a revolutionary development; it provided the basis for settled life in Meso-America. From these early agriculturists, the Toltec, Maya, and Aztec civilizations arose, and their peoples hybridized corn to increase yields, which in turn supported the growth of larger populations. They also cultivated beans, squashes, chile peppers, avocados, and potatoes. Agricultural technology included irrigation canals; artificial gardens that floated on water; and moisture-retention tillage, which allowed dry farming on nonirrigated lands.

The diet of early Meso-Americans was nutritionally complete, although it included little meat. Corn supplied carbohydrates, squashes and beans supplied vegetable proteins and nutrients, avocados provided essential fats and oils, and chiles supplied the essential vitamins A and C. And because these early Americans soaked their corn in lime, calcium and niacin were added to their diet. They also grew tobacco and several species of cotton. While commoners' diets were simple, nobles feasted on roasted turkey and quail as well as casseroles made with turkey, chiles, tomatoes, and ground pumpkin seeds.

Anthropologists have found evidence that beans were grown in the Andes as early as 5600 B.C. Farming provided the base on which the Incas and their predecessors built extraordinary civilizations. Approximately six thousand years ago, the early Andean farmers grew peanuts, white potatoes, and sweet potatoes. Of the hundreds of species of potatoes known today, many were developed by these early farmers. They also grew tomatoes, lima beans, chiles, and squashes. Some evidence suggests that Andean farmers may have domesticated corn more than five thousand years ago. The early Peruvian technology included stone hoes and digging sticks, irrigation systems, and the use of seagull manure, *guano,* to fertilize the fields. Because of these advanced farming practices, the little valleys on the rainless coast of Peru were able to support dense and highly distinctive populations for thousands of years.

Beginning in the thirteenth century, the Incas began conquering and consolidating the various peoples and nations of the Andes. Under the Inca Empire, land was farmed communally; crop yields were divided into three parts—one to sustain the local community, one to support the royal government of the Inca, and one to support the state religion—the worship of Inti—and its attendant priesthood. Surpluses were distributed to needy areas or stored against future need in government storehouses. To increase the land's productivity, government agencies collected and distributed *guano*

fertilizer from the offshore islands of Peru, and seagulls were declared protected by Inca law. As a result of the *guano,* Peruvian farmland yielded two crops a year. Stone walls were built to terrace whole mountainsides, and fertile soil was collected and moved up the mountains to enrich the planting areas. Elaborate systems of ditches and sluices brought water to the fields. Some of these mountain irrigation systems were fifty to seventy-five miles long and are considered major feats of engineering even today. Many of these same systems are, in fact, still in use. In desert regions, vast aqueducts were built to bring water from the mountains, as far as four hundred miles away, to form rich, productive oases.

Besides corn, potatoes, beans, chiles, and squashes, the early Peruvian diet also included pineapples, papayas, avocados, guinea pigs, *chicha* (corn beer), and ceremonial bread made from corn. Where it was too cold for corn—higher up in the Andes—quinoa, a high-protein grain, was grown. Llamas, domesticated thousands of years before and primarily raised as pack animals, also provided their owners with fertilizer, fuel, wool, and pelts. They were used as offerings for ritual sacrifice, and when they died naturally, they were eaten.

Many New World peoples profited from the agricultural innovations of the Andean and Meso-American agriculturists. Through trade, migration, and sometimes warfare, seeds and cuttings were dispersed throughout much of the hemisphere. On the settled islands of the Caribbean—Monserrat, for example—the original peoples dwelled in villages, where they lived by fishing and hunting and gathering. They maintained gardens in which they grew plants that had been originally domesticated primarily in South America and then improved over thousands of years by careful selection. Large cultivated plots included corn, peanuts, cassavas, pineapples, sweet potatoes, papayas, peppers, squashes, guavas, avocados, and a variety of New World beans as well as medicinal plants.

Along with improving their agricultural storehouse, early Americans also developed often unique ways of preparing and preserving their food items. These techniques evolved over the ages in response to the individual needs of each population.

Native American peoples had no large domestic animals to provide a ready source of cooking fat; their traditional cooking was relatively fat-free.

Lard—and deep-frying as a cooking method—were introduced by the Europeans along with the domestic pig. And while the early Americans did have some plant oils available to them—peanut oil in South America, corn oil in Central America, and sunflower oil in North America—it was not used extensively in cooking. The preferred methods of cooking included grilling and steaming. Leaves were often used by the Mayas to wrap foods for underground pit cooking. Achiote (annatto) seeds, sea salt, and chiles were used to flavor meats such as pheasant, venison, and fish. The central Mexicans used corn husks to wrap tamales for steaming. Comals—flat clay griddles—were used to cook tortillas. North American coastal peoples developed the clambake: Hot stones were placed in a cooking pit and layers of seaweed were alternated with corn, potatoes, clams, and lobsters. Caribs developed *boucan,* a style of barbecue: Meat was salted and smoke dried over a fire on lattices made of green wood.

Jerky (from the Quechuan word *charqui*) was developed by the Incas as a means of preserving the meat of game animals. Deboned and defatted meat was cut into one-quarter-inch-thick slices and then dipped into brine or rubbed with salt. The meat was then rolled up in the animal's hide for ten to twelve hours until the moisture was drawn out by the salt. The meat was then hung in the sun to dry in the cool, dehydrating breezes of the Andean altiplano. Finally, the finished product—jerky—was tied up in convenient bundles.

Pemmican (from the Cree word for fat) was made from drying thinly sliced, lean meat—usually from a large game animal such as a buffalo—over a fire or in the sun and wind. After drying, the meat was pounded to shreds and mixed thoroughly with an almost equal quantity of melted fat, some bone marrow, and a few handfuls of wild cherries. It was then packed in rawhide sacks and sealed with tallow.

Over the course of millennia, throughout the rise and ebb of many cultures, the peoples of the Americas developed a rich larder of fruits and vegetables, spices and condiments; and they perfected cooking methods and preservation techniques to best use this culinary array. This aggregation was the bounty of the Americas, the legacy of these pre-Columbian farmers which is dispersed throughout the world today.

So what culinary treasures did the Europeans bring back to the Old World? An inventory of the plant foods introduced to Europe, Asia, and Africa from the Americas includes the following:

Achiote

Allspice

Avocado

Beans (lima, pinto, pink, red, black, navy, great northern, green beans, etc.)

Brazil nut

Cactus pear

Cashew

Cassava

Chayote

Cherimoya

Chile

Chocolate

Corn

Filé

Guava

Jícama

Papaya

Passionfruit

Peanut

Pecan

Pineapple

Potato

Quinoa

Squash

Sunflower

Sweet potato

Tomatillo

Tomato

Vanilla

Wild rice

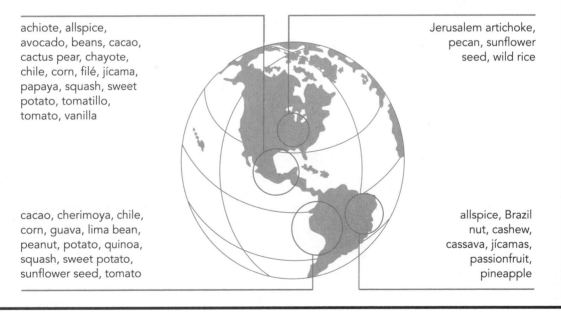

THE AMERICAN CORNUCOPIA

achiote, allspice, avocado, beans, cacao, cactus pear, chayote, chile, corn, filé, jícama, papaya, squash, sweet potato, tomatillo, tomato, vanilla

Jerusalem artichoke, pecan, sunflower seed, wild rice

cacao, cherimoya, chile, corn, guava, lima bean, peanut, potato, quinoa, squash, sweet potato, sunflower seed, tomato

allspice, Brazil nut, cashew, cassava, jícamas, passionfruit, pineapple

El Cocodrilo's Cookbook

Achiote

Achiote is made from the small brick-red seeds of the annatto tree. The powder form of the seeds is used by the food industry to give a yellow or orange color to butter, margarine, cheddar cheese, and smoked fish. Achiote paste, which is prepared from crushed achiote seeds and spices, imparts an earthy, smoky flavor to meats, fish, and poultry when the paste is rubbed on as a marinade coating before cooking. Besides being an important seasoning used in Mayan cooking, achiote is used as a body paint by tribal people. Red symbolizes courage and virility, so achiote paste is often used to paint faces, or as in the case of the Colorado people, to sculpt hair styles for the men. Tribal weavers use achiote to dye wool and other natural fibers a warm saffron-yellow color.

NOTE

Achiote can be found in Latin grocery stores. Achiote seeds are sold in small cellophane bags; they need to be ground before they can be used as a condiment. Achiote is also available as a paste: ground, mixed with spices and vinegar, and ready to use. Packaged in the shape of a small brick, achiote paste is sometimes called *recado colorado*. The paste is rubbed on chicken, pork, and fish before roasting or grilling and adds a spicy, smoky flavor to the dish. For a substitution see page 149.

Allspice

Allspice is the one true aromatic spice of the New World. The spice is produced from the small berries of the evergreen pimiento tree, a member of the myrtle family which grows wild in the Caribbean and the Amazon. When the Spanish explorers came across the berries, they named the spice *pimento* because the dried berries looked like large peppercorns. Though the Spaniards never found the wealth of spices they were seeking in the West Indies—the true cinnamon, cloves, black pepper, and nutmeg of the East—they did find in "allspice" a combination of the flavors of those prized spices. Today allspice is widely used in Caribbean cooking; in Jamaica, where it is still known as pimento, allspice forms the basis of the flavorful jerk seasoning.

Avocado

The avocado originated in Mexico and Guatemala and has been grown there for thousands of years. Later, its cultivation spread to South America, where it was grown by the pre-Incas. In Peru, archeologists have found avocado seeds and leaves, sometimes buried with mummies, dating back to 750 B.C. The Aztecs called the avocado *ahuacatl,* which means "testicle" (presumably because of the shape of the fruit), and believed—not surprisingly—that it was an aphrodisiac.

In pre-Columbian diets, which contained little meat, avocados provided an excellent dietary source of protein. Today, avocados are referred to as "poor man's butter" in the tropics because their creamy flesh contains twenty times as much fat as other fruits. Because avocados are members of the vegetable kingdom, this

NOTE

Also known as alligator pears, perhaps due to the rough texture of the green skin, avocados can be ripened by placing them in a paper bag and storing them in a warm place. When preparing avocados for a dish such as guacamole, you can keep them from turning brown by sprinkling the exposed flesh with fresh lemon or lime juice. If you have a choice, buy the dark, almost black rough-skinned Haas avocados (with their buttery, rich flavor and creamy texture) instead of the shiny, green smooth-skinned avocados (which have little flavor and a more watery texture).

"butter" is cholesterol free. The fruit ranges in size from a few ounces to four pounds and is rich in protein, minerals, and vitamins A and B. The leaves can be used to flavor stews, much as bay leaves are.

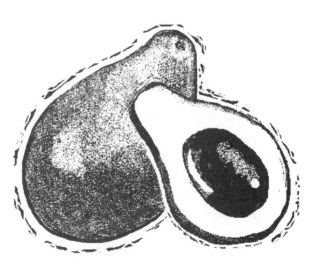

Beans

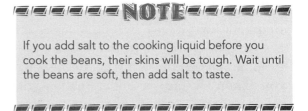

Beans are one of the oldest foods known to humankind, and for many peoples of the world today, they remain one of the main staffs of life. Lima beans were being grown in Peru nearly eight thousand years ago, and pre-Mayas were growing kidney beans seven thousand years ago in the Yucatán. Most varieties of beans known throughout the world today originated in the Americas or are varieties developed from American stock. The common green bean (also known as the snap or string bean), the lima bean, the wax bean, and all the familiar dried beans—kidney, pinto, navy, great northern, red, black, and pink—trace their heritage to the Western Hemisphere. Dried beans are a great source of protein and have no cholesterol and comparatively little fat.

Easily grown and stored, beans provided a major component of the ancient American diet. When the Spanish arrived in Mexico, they found that the Aztecs had a rainbow of colored beans available. The remains of foods that are preserved in ancient ruins leave clues to

NOTE

If you add salt to the cooking liquid before you cook the beans, their skins will be tough. Wait until the beans are soft, then add salt to taste.

their role in the lives of early peoples. Native Americans must have considered beans to be very important, because they have been found as sacrificial food offerings. For example, the mummy of a young boy, sacrificed by the Incas, was found on the slopes of the volcano Aconcagua. Carefully wrapped and dressed, he had been provided with a pair of sandals and two bags: One was empty, but the other contained cooked beans—a meal for the child's journey into the next life.

Beans retain their nutritional importance throughout the world today, especially in areas where meat and dairy products are unavailable, or are too costly for families to buy. Versatile and filling, dried beans are an excellent source of protein, calcium, phosphorus, and iron.

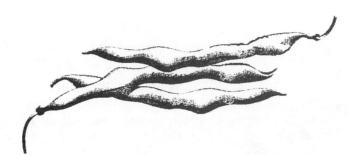

Brazil Nut

Brazil nuts are gathered by tribal peoples and peasant collectors from the trees that are scattered throughout the rain forest of the Amazon Basin. During the annual harvest, the round pods fall to the ground from the giant Brazil nut trees. These extremely hard capsules are about the size of a softball and contain the seeds of the tree. A falling Brazil nut pod can easily kill a person. The woody pods are so hard that they have to be hacked open with a machete before the nuts can be removed. The nuts are dried in wooden shacks before they are sold. The income gained from Brazil nuts provides many forest dwellers with their biggest source of income.

The sale of Brazil nuts brings millions of dollars a year into the international market. Attempts to grow the nuts on plantations have failed—for while the tree grows well and flowers, it produces no nuts. It seems that while no one knows for sure how Brazil nuts are pollinated, those trees that produce nuts are visited regularly by euglossine bees. These bees require the pheromones from a certain species of epiphytic orchids in order to mate

NOTE

Brazil nuts gathered in the wild have given rise to cooperatives that are owned and operated by forest peoples. This provides the native harvesters with three to ten times the normal income for their labor. Because Brazil nuts have not been successfully domesticated, the income from wild nut harvesting provides an incentive to preserve and protect the rain forest. Hopefully, as demand for Brazil nuts grows, people will realize that it is more profitable to harvest the rain forest's renewable wealth than to cut the trees down for short-term profits.

and reproduce. (Pheromones are fragrance chemicals used by animals to communicate with others of the same species.) These particular orchids in turn rely exclusively on the euglossine bees for pollination. So, without the euglossine orchids, there are no euglossine bees; and without the euglossine bees, the flowers of the Brazil nut trees remain unpollinated and so, of course, the trees are barren.

Another forest animal, the agouti, has a role in the propagation of wild Brazil nut trees. After the ripe seed capsule falls to the forest floor, the trees depend on the agouti, a rabbit-size rodent, to crack open the hard casing so the seeds can germinate.

Like all biospheres, the rain forest is a complex network of interdependent plants, insects, and animals woven together to support an ecosystem that has evolved over millennia. If one factor is removed—say the bee or the agouti—the balance of nature will be upset and the overall well-being and regeneration of the rain forest will be affected.

Cactus Pear

Cactus pears, or prickly pears, are the fruit of the nopal cactus—the one with the paddle-shaped "leaves." About the size of a large egg, the pears are, in fact, big, spine-covered berries. Originally native to northwest Mexico and the southwest United States, cactus pears provided prehistoric peoples with fruits in the desert. With the arrival of the Europeans, the nopal cactus was exported and planted abroad. People enjoy its fruit all over the Mediterranean area; the southern part of Africa; and Australia, southwestern Asia, and Central and South America. Cactus pears, in fact, are more popular and appreciated abroad than they are here in their native United States.

NOTE

Because of their vivid magenta color, cactus pears make wonderful, tropical-looking drinks. Mix the fruit with lemon juice and sugar and then purée; sieve the seeds, chill, and use the liquid as a base for rum, gin, or vodka. Cactus pear purée can be used to make sorbets, jams, or added to fruit smoothies.

Cactus pears have a sweet, soft, grainy pulp. In Latin America, where many varieties of the fruit are available, cactus pears come in an incredible array of colors: cut them open and you'll find red, violet, pink, yellow, chartreuse, and ocher flesh. Since the cactus pears are covered with often invisible hair-like stickers, be careful when peeling the rind.

Cactus pears are seasonal; they can be found in Mexican markets and some specialty produce stores from fall through spring. The fruit sold in the United States is most commonly a medium green to dark magenta on the outside; the seedy interior flesh varies in color from a yellow gold to a deep magenta red. Choose fruit with a full, deep, even color. It should be tender and yielding, but not mushy. Cactus pears will ripen at room temperature and, when ripe, can be stored in the refrigerator for about a week.

Cashew

The cashew is an evergreen shrub native to the West Indies and Brazil. It produces a red- or yellow-skinned fruit called the marañon, which resembles a pear-shaped apple. Out of the end of this bitter, acidic fruit grows the kidney-shaped cashew nut. The shell of the nut is so toxic it is hard to believe a simple roasting process removes the deadly toxins, along with the shells, leaving a delicious buttery nut. For many peoples in the Amazon, cashews are a source of income as well as an essential part of their diet. For some, like the Tupí, cashews are actually the principal staple of their diet, so the trees are highly valued, occasionally causing tribal warfare. Some Amazon peoples believe that the regular chewing of cashews prevents tooth decay, and the juice of the fruit is thought to stimulate the brain, improve memory, and relieve fatigue. Cashews are also used to treat dysentery. Some Amazon people believe that a diet exclusively of cashews will cure illnesses such as leprosy and diabetes.

The Portuguese in Brazil recognized the value of the cashew early on and exported trees to colonies in Goa, Madagascar, Mozambique, and Angola. In Africa and India, the fruits and nuts became an important part of local diets where marañon and cashews are now used in sauces, drinks, and sweets.

Today, there is a worldwide market not only for the delicious nuts of the cashew tree but also for the by-products, which include oil and a lacquer that offers protection to wood against insects and fungus. Cashew oil, in fact, is used in at least one hundred industrial patents.

Cassava

Cassava (*cas-sav'-ah*) is the edible tuber of a plant native to the Brazilian Amazon; it's a relative of the poinsettia. Many North Americans are unfamiliar with cassava, though they are well acquainted with one of its products: tapioca. The long, narrow cassava tubers are covered with thick, rough, dark brown skin. When the skin is removed, the flesh inside is dense, white, and fibrous. Called yuca in Central America and manioc in parts of South America, cassava is a staple of many ethnic cuisines throughout tropical America and the Caribbean. The sweet, starchy tubers are used in soups and stews as potatoes would be; they're also made into fritters, chips, flat bread, dumplings, and breads. Cassava can be fried, grilled, and steamed.

In the Amazon, the traditional cyanide-laden wild cassava was used as poison for arrowheads and blowgun darts. After the cyanide was leached out (the tuber was peeled and grated, and the poisonous juices squeezed out under pressure), cassava was used as a base for beer. In many traditional cultures today, cassava still remains the popular base for beer.

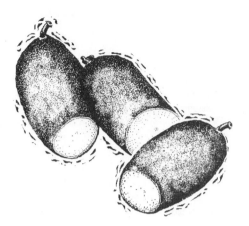

Grated, boiled, and leached of any poisons, the cassava is chewed—salivary enzymes convert starch to sugar—then put into a large pot with water where it ferments. Beer from cassava contributes a significant amount of vitamin B to the diets of tribal peoples.

During the sixteenth century, European travelers noted that Native Caribbean peoples made cassava into bread. After leaching the tubers of cyanide, the tuber was sieved and the pulp was shaped into cakes. The cakes were cooked on griddles. The Portuguese brought the root to Africa where it also became a staple—it's resistant to locusts and can be left in the ground for up to two years past maturity as a hedge against hunger. Crop breeders in Nigeria have recently developed an improved variety of cassava, which could double the output of the crop and help fight famine in Africa since it can thrive in poor soils and is resistant to drought. Because the cassava is inexpensive, a growing number of middle-class homes in central and western Africa are beginning to turn from the more costly rice and yams to cassava, which can be eaten whole, grated, or fermented, and used to make various traditional dishes.

Chayote

Also known as a "vegetable pear," the chayote (*cha-yo'-tee*) is the size and shape of a large pear—a pear which appears to have been gently flattened in a vice. The *chayotli* was cultivated by the ancient Mayas and Aztecs and was one of their principal food crops. Chayote grows prolifically on vines: one vine can produce more than a hundred chayotes and a myriad of nectar-rich, honey-producing blossoms. Green and squashlike in taste and texture, botanists refer to chayotes as "one-seeded cucumbers." Called a *chocho* in Jamaica, *mirliton* in Louisiana, and *christophene* in France, chayote can be prepared much like zucchini: It can be grated raw into salads, stuffed and baked, sautéed, steamed, or stir-fried. The large central seed of a young chayote can also be cooked along with the chayote, then enjoyed separately; it's edible and tasty.

NOTE

Chayotes are found in large supermarkets and in Latin and Oriental markets, especially during the wintertime. Choose firm, unblemished small fruits as they are the most tender. They can be stored for up to a month, lightly wrapped, in the refrigerator. If you buy the large chayotes, you will need to peel the skin—either before cooking with a potato peeler or after cooking by pulling the skin off.

Cherimoya

The cherimoya originated in the Andes of Ecuador and Peru; prized by the pre-Columbian farmers, its name means "fruit of the cold country" in Quechua. Pottery representations of cherimoya have been found in archeological sites dating back to pre-Inca times. From South America, cultivation of the fruit spread north to Central America and the Caribbean. Sometimes called custard apples—because you can eat them with a spoon—cherimoyas have the flavor and texture of a creamy, tropical strawberry mousse. The fruit contains a full cargo of inedible shiny, hard, black seeds that feel nice to the tongue, like polished river rocks. The cherimoya has been described as looking like a "Stone Age artichoke" because its leathery green skin is covered with scalelike impressions.

Because the female blossom of the cherimoya is so narrow, only a very tiny, night-flying insect exclusive to South America can pollinate this blossom. Cherimoya trees now being cultivated in lands where the insect does not exist must be pollinated by hand. This entails collecting the pollen from a male blossom with

NOTE

Available winter through spring, cherimoyas weigh between one-half and two pounds. Look for a fruit that is firm and green and devoid of any dark or splotchy marks. Cherimoyas bruise easily in spite of their leathery skins, so be careful. The fruit will ripen at room temperature; when ripe, its skin will turn a darker green and yield to slight pressure. Don't let the cherimoya get overly ripe; refrigerate it when it's ready, or it will be mushy. Cherimoyas are best served halved and eaten with a spoon (discard the seeds as you go). The fruit can also be seeded and puréed and made into sauces for desserts, tropical drinks, and smoothies.

very fine-tipped watercolor brushes and then introducing the pollen to the female blossoms. To complicate matters, the female blossoms are receptive only during a twenty-four-hour period, and not all blossoms on the same tree are ready on the same day.

Chile

The first chiles were tiny berries that grew on vines beneath the canopy of the Amazon rain forest thousands of years ago. One of the first plants cultivated in the New World, chiles, wild and domesticated, have been used by American peoples for at least eight thousand years. Evidence shows that by 5500 B.C. the Tehuacanos in Mexico were growing their own; early chile cultivation in Peru dates back to about 2000 B.C. By the time Columbus traveled to the New World, chiles had been used by the Inca, Olmec, Toltec, Maya, Aztec, and other nations to add spice and flavor to their cooking. Chiles, high in vitamin C, were used

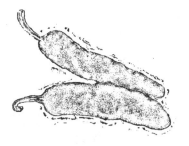

in sauces, cooked with meat or fish dishes, used in soups and stews, mixed with salt and tomatoes, and sprinkled on foods as a condiment.

Chiles also played an important medicinal role in the healing arts of the Mayas. Chiles were taken internally to treat asthma and stubborn coughs, used externally as a paste to treat aching bones and muscles, and applied as a poultice for sore throats. Even today, some over-the-counter heat rubs contain as a principal active ingredient capsaicin, the chemical in chiles that is responsible for the hot sensation.

Though chiles are now associated with many international ethnic cuisines—Szechwan, Indian, Thai, Korean, and Hungarian, to name a few—it was Columbus who introduced this New World spice to the Old World. Within fifty years after Columbus's voyage, the use of chiles was widespread. Shops carried a variety of peppers; they were grown in gardens and used both as food and as medicine. The Portuguese introduced them to Asia, where as early as 1542 three varieties were reported growing in Goa on the coast of India. By the seventeenth century, hot peppers were common in the most remote parts of the world. By the eighteenth century, the use of chiles in Oriental cuisine was so commonplace that it was assumed that chiles were native to Asia.

Ethnobotanists reason that chiles were welcomed by many different cultures because their flavor spiced up the sometimes bland food in often limited native diets, masked the "off" flavors of food kept too long without refrigeration, or, as the Chinese found, even added a lift to already highly seasoned food. Chiles also grow easily in most warm climates and seeds saved from one or two pods could provide a year's crop for a whole family. And while those eating chiles were unaware of the nutritional benefits, chiles provided vitamins A and C to diets lacking these essential ingredients. Chile eaters probably just felt better than their neighbors —and it is from this kind of observation and awareness, without knowledge of the scientific basis, that the body of nutritional folk wisdom has developed.

Today, there are at least two hundred varieties of chiles—one hundred of them indigenous to Mexico. They range in heat from the sweet bell pepper to the lethally hot habanero, in shape from the skinny ají to the plump manzano, and in length from the tiny one-quarter-inch macho to the nine-inch chilaca. Chiles cover the spectrum of colors from green through yellow, orange, red, purple, and brown to almost black.

NOTE

Chiles are great for diets: They're high in vitamins A and C, and have next to no calories or fat; they increase salivation, improve digestion, and make food taste better. And, according to recent claims by scientists in Japan and the United Kingdom, eating chiles causes the body to burn up to 25 percent more calories during the day than it normally would. To top this, researchers are now claiming that capsaicin may act as an antibiotic, speed healing in wounds, stop pain when applied as an ointment to wounds, and have anticancer effects by preventing the liver from turning some elements into carcinogens.

Chocolate

Cocoa beans are native to South America; they were brought into Mexico by the Mayas before A.D. 600. The beans grow in seedpods on wide-branched evergreen trees; each pod contains up to forty beans. The pre-Aztecs considered cocoa of divine origin and an important part of the diet of their god, Quetzalcoatl. The Aztecs, Toltecs, Totonacs, as well as the Mayas, ground the cocoa beans into a paste on a grinding stone and blended it with allspice, cinnamon, or vanilla; sometimes it was spiced with chiles, sometimes it was colored with achiote to give it a reddish tint. The mixture was added to hot water, beaten, then served hot and frothy. The word chocolate comes from the Aztec *xocolatl,* which means "bitter water." To the Aztecs, cocoa was considered a special drink reserved only for nobles.

Cocoa beans themselves were used as currency in the Aztec Empire. They were bagged in standard quantities, and the price of goods was quoted in the number of beans required to make the purchase. In fact, until 1887, cocoa beans remained an accepted means of paying one's taxes in Mexico.

A craze hit Europe when chocolate was introduced; there it was drunk hot with milk and sugar. Later, a whole new school of confectionery art and expertise developed around chocolate making, and chocolate became one of the Western world's sweetest addictions.

Corn

Corn made the ancient American civilizations of the Inca, Maya, and Aztec—and those of North America—possible. Corn was the basis of life and civilization for these cultures; it played a profound role in their art, architecture, religion, and family relationships. Corn was sacred and became the metaphor for all the basic processes of life; it was central to ceremonies, the cycles of life and death, fertility, growth, and renewal. Each culture had corn gods, and the arrival of corn into each culture was celebrated with myths and legends of gods, goddesses, or sacred animals bringing it to humans. For many Native Americans today, corn remains the most sacred food.

Sometime around 2500 B.C., the ancient peoples of America domesticated corn from wild grasses by deliberate cultivation of the seeds. These early agriculturists not only domesticated corn but actually created the plant as we know it today. Cultivated forms spread from tribe to tribe through South, Central, and North America. Since corn must be hand planted, its cultivation meant the end of nomadic life and the beginning of stable societies, which in turn produced several major civilizations. Through breeding, corn has, in fact, become probably the only food plant that requires human help to reproduce— the impenetrable husk must be removed, or the sprouting kernels, crowded together on the cob, will choke to death.

Corn contains incomplete protein and lacks certain vitamins, but Native Americans combined it with beans and occasionally fish, which rounded out their protein require-ments. Some cultures processed it with lime or wood ash, which released the niacin stored in the kernel. Chiles and tomatoes added other missing vitamins to the early American diets. Native Mexicans began their day with a hot bowl of *atole,* or corn mush, sweetened with honey or spiced with chile. The main meal of the day, eaten in the early afternoon, consisted of tortillas, beans, and a sauce of tomatoes or peppers. Occasionally, the dishes might contain grubs, insect eggs, or pond algae. Tamales combined corn meal dough with beans, chiles, green tomato shavings, and shreds of meat or fish, all wrapped in a dried corn husk and steamed.

During Columbus's first voyage to the New World, corn fields stretched up to eighteen miles long in Cuba. When Columbus tasted corn, he pronounced it "most tasty boiled, roasted, or ground into flour." He brought corn seeds back to Europe with him in 1493, and within a few years, the Spanish had introduced corn around the Mediterranean. By the mid-sixteenth century, corn had become familiar enough to Europeans to become the basis of such national dishes as Italian polenta and Romanian

mamaliga. Corn was also adopted by the Philippine islanders and some Asian peoples. In Africa, it was found that corn grew more rapidly than other grains and needed very little cultivation. Because corn weathered drought and the harsh African sun better than other staple foods, it was often the only food consumed by some families.

While there are many varieties of corn, the most common are popcorn, dent corn (for feeding animals), sweet corn (for roasting on the ear and eating), and flint corn (for making grits and masa, the flour for tortillas and tamales).

Filé

The Choctaws originally gathered the young leaves of the sassafras trees that grew wild in the bayous along the Gulf of Mexico. They dried the leaves and ground them into a powder to make a seasoning for their cooking. After the arrival of the European settlers, this seasoning, called filé, was sold in the marketplaces of New Orleans. Filé became an important ingredient in Louisiana cooking and was used as a flavoring and thickener for Creole soups such as gumbo. Filé powder, which tastes like sassafras and has an earthy flavor, is available in supermarkets and gourmet specialty stores. It is often labeled "gumbo filé."

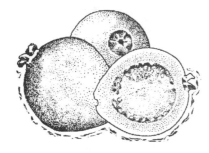

Guava

$\wedge\wedge\wedge\wedge\wedge\wedge\wedge\wedge\wedge\wedge\wedge\wedge\wedge\wedge\wedge\wedge\wedge$

Native to South America, the guava has been domesticated for thousands of years—archeologists have reported evidence of preserved guavas dating back to 2500 B.C. in coastal Peru.

Guavas are members of the aromatic myrtle family, which includes cloves, allspice, and eucalyptus. There are many varieties of guavas. About two inches in diameter, guavas are actually juicy berries—round or pear-shaped—that grow on thirty-foot trees. Their seedy, reddish-pink flesh has a rather gritty texture, which is probably why the Aztecs called the guava *xalxocotl,* or "sand pear." Guavas are available during summer months. Tart yet sweet, guavas will ripen at room temperature; as they ripen they will begin to exude a rich tropical fragrance. While varieties of guavas vary in flavor, all of them are intensely aromatic. When they're ready to eat, they will yield to light fingertip pressure. They can be peeled and eaten (the seeds are said to be good for the digestion) or used in fruit salads, or for making sauces, preserves, or pie fillings.

Guavas are prized in Latin America for making a sweet, dark red paste called *guayabate* —a popular dessert which is eaten like candy or served with a slice of cheese—and for making fragrant, refreshing fruit drinks.

Jerk

$\wedge\wedge\wedge\wedge\wedge\wedge\wedge\wedge\wedge\wedge\wedge\wedge\wedge\wedge\wedge\wedge\wedge$

Jerk is a popular method of barbecuing well-seasoned pork, chicken, or fish. It has given rise to a thriving roadside industry in Jamaica where the jerked meat is cooked over coals in mobile steel-drum furnaces. Originally developed by the Arawaks in the Caribbean, the seasoning and smoking of meats was later perfected by runaway Jamaican slaves and their descendants, called Maroons. Fiercely independent, the Maroons persisted for more than two hundred years in the harsh, remote mountain areas in the center of the island, repelling all efforts to dislodge them. Having learned the art of preserving meat from the Arawaks, the Maroons improved on the Native American technique. The result was jerk—a highly spiced and aromatic seasoning combination that includes a goodly amount of salt. Jerk was slathered on meats, which were then cooked very slowly over a green-wood fire or in a stone-lined pit. Today, jerk is a signature flavor in Jamaican cooking, and it is used to give a highly flavorful zing to chicken, fish, and meat.

Jícama

A jícama (*hee'-kah-mah*) resembles a fat turnip with sandy brown skin. This tropical American root vegetable has a crisp white flesh; its taste and texture are much like a cross between an apple and a water chestnut. Jícamas are native to Mexico and the headwaters of the Amazon River. The Spanish introduced the jícama to the Philippines in the seventeenth century, and from there its cultivation spread throughout Asia and the Pacific. Today, jícamas are a popular snack food in Mexico; crunchy, juicy slices of jícama are eaten with a sprinkle of chile powder and a squeeze of lime juice.

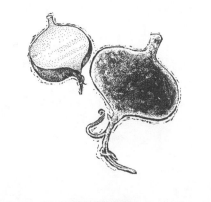

NOTE

Jícamas are becoming more common in supermarkets and in Latin and Oriental markets. The smooth, thin-skinned tubers with juicy—not woody—flesh underneath are the freshest. (To check for freshness, make a tiny scrape in the skin with your fingernail.) Jícamas, uncut and unwrapped, will keep for weeks in the refrigerator. Used in salsas, salads, and stir-fries, low-fat jícamas stay crunchy even when cooked—so they add few calories to a dish but a lot of bite.

NOTE

In the United States, papayas are usually harvested when they are green; they will ripen, but never with the wonderful full flavor of the tropical tree-ripened varieties. Most of the papayas available in supermarkets come from Hawaii; these small, yellow, pear-shaped papayas weigh about one pound. Papayas ripen from the blossom end of the fruit up to the stem end; as the fruit ripens, the green skin turns to a mixture of green, yellow and orange. A ripe Hawaiian papaya will be bright yellow. When ripe, the papaya gives off a fruity aroma and will yield to light pressure.

Papaya

The papaya is native to the tropical lowlands of Central America. The tree itself is a tall, smooth, unbranched trunk with a parasol of leaves stemming out of the top. Amazingly this tree can grow from a seed to a fruit-bearing tree in little over a year. Often called a melon tree, the soft, fragrant, melonlike fruits of the papaya, which can reach twenty pounds each, grow directly out of the leafless trunk of the tree. The latex of the green fruit contains *papain*, a protein digestive enzyme that is used as a meat tenderizer. The pungent seeds of the papaya are edible and said to be a digestive aid; they make a great garnish or addition to salad dressing. Rich in vitamins A and C, the rosy, pumpkin-yellow flesh of the papaya is sweet and fragrant with an earthy aftertaste.

Passionfruit

Native to Brazil, the passionfruit vine was so named by early Spanish explorers because its large, red flower seemed to contain various symbols of Christ's crucifixion, or Passion. To these men, the five petals and five sepals represented the ten Apostles present at the crucifixion, the corona of fine filaments resembled the crown of thorns, the five stamens represented the five wounds in Christ's body, and the three stigmas stood for the nails used in the crucifixion. The explorers interpreted the flower as symbolic of Christ's approval of their missionary work in the New World.

Passionfruit is an oval berry, about the size of a large egg; the variety known as the purple passionfruit comes with leathery, purple-brown skin. The flesh is slippery and jelly like, and is contained in little sacks which are attached around a multitude of seeds. This juicy golden flesh is sweet and tangy at the same time, with a rich, floral fragrance. The juice of

NOTE

The rind of ripe passionfruit has the dimpled surface texture of a golf ball; it's dark, wrinkled, and dented. Passionfruit ripen at room temperature. If the fruit is firm and smooth, the passionfruit is not yet ripe; when the rind yields to slight fingertip pressure, and liquid can be heard moving inside, then it's ready to be eaten. Refrigerate ripe passionfruits for up to a week (or freeze them in plastic bags). Passionfruits can be eaten as they are—seeds and all—or sieve the seeds and use the fragrant pulp as flavoring for sorbets, mousses, ice creams, tropical drinks, fruit sauces, or meat marinades.

the passionfruit, popular as a refreshing drink in the tropics, is just beginning to be introduced to the United States as an ingredient in commercial fruit juice blends. Ornamental varieties of the passionfruit vine can be seen growing in warmer areas of the United States such as Florida and California.

Peanut

VVVVVVVVVVVVVVVVVV

Peanuts were first domesticated in their native South America. They have been found sealed in vases in ancient Peruvian tombs dating back to 1500 B.C. Later, the Incas used peanuts in religious ceremonies and in burial rites; pots of peanuts were buried with their mummified dead—sometimes cradled in their arms—to nourish their spirits on their way to the afterlife.

The Spanish introduced peanuts to the Malay Archipelago after first encountering them in Haiti and Peru. In the early 1600s, peanuts became a component part of several Asian mainland ethnic cuisines. Portuguese sailors coming from Brazil introduced peanuts to Africa. When Africans were brought to the New World as slaves, they brought peanuts with them and "reintroduced" them to this hemisphere. Although Native Americans had cultivated peanuts in Virginia before the arrival of the European colonists, it was the Africans who were responsible for the widespread cultivation of peanuts in North America, calling them by their Bantu name *nguba* (ground nut), which the colonists rendered as "goober."

Peanuts are not really nuts, but a member of the legume (pea) family. They grow underground and actually are seeds encased in a nutlike shell. After the plant's flowers have been fertilized, the flower stalk elongates and forces the growing seedpod underground where it grows to maturity. Peanuts are high in niacin, zinc, protein, fat, and fiber, but, like all members of the vegetable kingdom, they contain no cholesterol.

Pecan

VVVVVVVVVVVVVVVVVV

The pecan, meaning boneshell, gets its name from the combination of several North American languages: the Algonquin *paccan,* the Cree *pakan,* and the Abinaki *pagan.* A species of hickory tree, native to Oklahoma and the Mississippi River Valley, the pecan was prized by indigenous American peoples. During a trek to western Mexico in 1528, the explorer Cabeza de Vaca noted that tribes along the Gulf of Mexico gathered together along river bottoms to eat the nuts. They also extracted a milky fluid from pecans and hickories, which they used in making corn cakes.

Many tribes used pecans extensively, either mixed with beans, cooked with fruits, pressed into oils, ground into a meal to thicken stews, or roasted. Pecans have the highest fat content of all nuts, 70 percent, and also have a high caloric content.

Pecan pralines are traditionally associated with old New Orleans. Originally, pralines were a French creation made with almonds; they were Americanized in Louisiana by substituting the Old World nuts for New World pecans. In the evenings, Creole women would walk along the streets selling these sweet pralines from straw baskets.

Pineapple

A member of the bromelaid family, pineapples have been cultivated for at least eight hundred years in South America. Symbolic representations of its form were found in pre-Incan ruins. When the Tupí-Guaraní spread outward from the Paraná–Paraguay Basin, they brought the pineapple with them; through trade, they introduced the fruit to other peoples.

When Columbus landed at Guadeloupe in the Lesser Antilles, he found the local inhabitants cultivating pineapples. The Caribs called the plant *anana,* which means "fragrance" or "fragrant fruit" in Tupí-Guaraní. The Spaniards thought that the fruit, growing out of a rosette of leathery, spiked leaves, looked like a large pinecone, so they called it a piña de los Indias (Indian pinecone) or piña, for short. (The English later added the word *apple,* a generic term for fruit.) The Caribs used pineapples as symbols of hospitality, fastening them over doorways as a welcoming sign for visitors. The Europeans adopted this symbolic use of the fruit and it became a feature on shields and crests, door knockers and bedposts, gates, and corners of buildings. The pineapple was also adopted as a sign of friendship in colonial North America. As a food item, the fruit was used fresh; as a garnish; or to soften tough, smoked meat.

When introduced to the European continent, pineapples set off a mini-rage among the upper classes. Because of its popularity with royalty and its regal appearance, with its crown of leaves on a large golden head, the pineapple became known as the king of fruits.

Potato

By 3000 B.C., potatoes were being grown by primitive farmers in the Andes of Peru; over the centuries, several hundred varieties of potatoes—including an array of colors, sizes, and shapes—were eventually developed by Native American farmers. Potatoes were an especially important crop above eleven thousand feet where corn would not grow. So important is the potato in the daily lives of Andean people, there are about two hundred words in the Amayra language to distinguish between the sizes, colors, and textures of this sustaining tuber.

The gene bank of the Centro Nacional de la Papa in La Molina, Peru, has samples of five thousand native potato cultivars (cultivated variations of species) from nine countries in South America, and of these, thirty-five hundred are genotypes (unique and separate subspecies of potatoes).

Since ancient times, Andean farmers have made *chuño,* a freeze-dried form of potatoes that keeps for months or indefinitely if ground into meal. *Chuño* is made in June when, at elevations above twelve thousand feet, the days are warm and sunny but the night temperatures drop below freezing. Small potatoes are spread on the ground to freeze overnight; then they are thawed in the morning sun. After thawing, the potatoes are gathered into little piles, and men and women tread on them with bare feet, squeezing out the moisture that has been released from the potato cells by the freezing process. The potatoes are then spread out to dry in the hot sun and eventually stored.

Potatoes, carried in the hulls of ships returning from the Americas, were introduced through various ports in Europe during the sixteenth century. They were met with varying degrees of acceptance. At first the tubers were considered poisonous since they were a member of the nightshade family; most people wouldn't eat them. Then for a time, the European elite thought potatoes cured impotence, causing a sharp increase in the perceived value and price of potatoes. While Spain, Switzerland, and the Lowland countries were growing potatoes by the mid-sixteenth century, they were banned in Burgundy in 1619 because it was thought that eating too many would cause leprosy. Fear of the unfamiliar prompted starving peasants in Kohlberg in 1774 to refuse to eat the potatoes that Frederick the Great sent the famine-afflicted city and the poor of Munich in 1795 to refuse the potatoes added to soup in the city's soup kitchen.

War and political upheaval as well as the military requisitioning of grain crops caused peasants to take a second look at potatoes. No other food crop could produce as many calories per acre; and when left in the ground, the vegetable couldn't be taken by soldiers or trampled or burned during times of war. Peasants learned how to cultivate the tuber and how to cook it. With time, the potato became recognized and accepted throughout Europe as a good subsistence crop. In the eighteenth century, potatoes planted in England and Ireland became the staple of poor farmers. Ireland became particularly dependent on the potato; the peasant diet there often consisted of potatoes and little else. In Russia, Catherine the Great promoted potatoes as an antidote to famine so

◀▬◀▬◀▬◀▬NOTE▬▶▬▶▬▶▬▶

Potatoes that are exposed to light for long periods of time will develop a greenish tinge on their skins that extends into the flesh; this is caused by the toxin solanin. Solanin can cause digestive disturbances if eaten. Always store potatoes in a cool, dark place where light cannot reach them. If you notice a green tinge on the skins, cut or scrape that part off of the potato before using it.

well that the national drink became vodka. By 1806, recipes for potatoes appeared for the first time in a French cookbook.

Because so many people depended on potato crops for subsistence, when the potato blight hit Europe in 1845, it was a human disaster. The blight completely destroyed crops and seed plants for the coming year; there was no way for a family to sustain itself or its livestock. Ireland was especially hard hit; disease racked the population and more than one million people died. Spurred by the famine, another million managed to immigrate to the United States, adding a significant new component to the social and economic makeup of the developing nation.

Potatoes are a great nutritional bargain: they're high in potassium, a good source of complex carbohydrates, and contain goodly amounts of vitamins C and B_6 and assorted minerals, and they're low in calories, unless you slather on the butter (only 120 calories in an average 6-ounce potato).

Quinoa

Quinoa (*keen'-wa*) is a high-protein grain that has been cultivated in the Andes for centuries. Ancient farmers found that quinoa could be grown above the tree line and up to the snow line, where more temperate crops such as corn could not grow. This nutritious grain was a staple of the ancient Inca, who called it the "mother grain"; it provided fuel for their powerful, conquering armies. Quinoa remains an important element in South American cooking. Andean people today use quinoa in making flour and for thickening stews and soups. The tiny golden seeds of this grain—they look like sesame seeds—cook up shiny and translucent, and offer complete protein, containing all eight essential amino acids. Many people today consider quinoa the super grain of the future because of its nutritional content.

Squash

Squashes are fruits of various members of the gourd family; they come in a variety of colors, shapes, and sizes. Early Americans domesticated summer squash between five and seven thousand years ago, and many of the varieties we are familiar with today have been cultivated in the Americas since that time. Rich in folic acid, potassium, and vitamin C, squash was an important ingredient in the diet of Native Americans.

Originally, the earliest squashes contained inedible flesh; they were grown for their large seeds, which contained highly nutritious oils and could be kept in baskets for an extended period of time. The squash seeds could be eaten or ground and used as thickeners in cooking, a technique that is still used today in Mexican cuisine. Eventually, the Native American plant breeders developed squashes with edible flesh. These squashes, such as zucchini, yellow crookneck, and pumpkin, became major food sources for early Americans. And as an important plus, the winter squash varieties—acorn, buttercup, pumpkin, butternut, and Hubbard—protected by their hard skins, could be stored for several months, providing the people with a hedge against hunger.

Relatives of the squash, gourds also proved very serviceable to early Americans. For thousands of years dried gourds served as handy and useful containers for water; they also provided a vehicle for artistic expression. Even today, gourd carving is an art. In rural areas, dried gourds are intricately carved with animal and village motifs or made into ceremonial masks.

Today, the calabasa, a bright orange squash, is part of the daily fare of many people in Central and South America and in the Caribbean.

This huge squash is sold by the piece in open-air marketplaces and used in soups and stews.

Sunflower

The Incas of Peru used to worship the sunflower, believing that it symbolized the sun. When the Spanish invaded Peru, they took home with them gold medallions shaped like sunflowers—and they also took home sunflower seeds. Soon Europeans fell in love with the bright yellow flower, and by the eighteenth century, it had become the centerpiece of many gardens.

The flowers, a ring of bright yellow petals resembling the sun's corona encircling a dark center of seeds, can reach twelve inches in diameter and grow on stems up to fifteen feet high. These blooms, almost mystically, always turn their faces toward the sun and slowly follow its path as it traces its arc across the sky.

Sunflower seeds are very rich in iron and are 24 percent protein by weight; their oil is high in polyunsaturated fat and low in saturated fat. Sunflowers were perhaps the first crop cultivated by dwellers of the North American plains. In 1605, the French explorer Champlain found Native Americans on the East Coast of North America cultivating the tubers of one species of sunflowers. The natives called them "sunroots." These tubers, now called Jerusalem artichokes or sun chokes, made a hit in seventeenth-century Europe when they were introduced. Fresh and crisp like water chestnuts, with a nutty potato-like flavor, Jerusalem artichokes are a versatile, iron-rich vegetable that can be eaten raw in snacks or salads, or baked, steamed, boiled, sautéed, or stir-fried.

Sweet Potato

∧∧∧∧∧∧∧∧∧∧∧∧∧∧∧∧

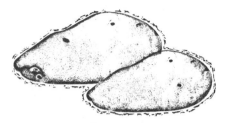

The sweet potato originated in Central America, then was carried to South America, where it was cultivated as early as 1000 B.C. A member of the morning glory family, the sweet potato plant produces long, edible tubers that are extremely rich in vitamin A and contain a fair amount of protein and vitamin C. Commonly mistaken for the sweeter yams, sweet potatoes are fluffier and more delicately flavored.

Columbus initially came across sweet potatoes on his first voyage. He, too, thought sweet potatoes were yams because he called them *niames,* from the West African name for yams. In a letter from a later voyage, Columbus described how sweet potatoes tasted like parsnips when eaten raw in salads and how they tasted like squash when cooked with pork, and he raved about how delicious sweet potatoes were when soaked in the milk of almonds. Today, sweet potatoes are eaten throughout Central and South America and the Caribbean in the form of breads, soups, candy, puffs, rolls, pies, potato chips, and tarts. Sweet potatoes, more than any other root vegetable, are the primary crop for many developing countries.

NOTE

Dr. Dean Edell reports that the Center for Science in the Public Interest set out to identify the most nutritious vegetable. Each vegetable received a score based on its percentage of U.S. Recommended Dietary Allowances (RDA) for six nutrients plus its fiber content. The winner, with 582 points, was the sweet potato. The sweet potato is high in ß-carotene, which is the precursor of vitamin A (essential for maintaining night vision and resistance to infection). The sweet potato is also high in vitamin C, which builds connective tissue fiber; folate, which allows normal growth and maintenance of the body's cells; calcium, which maintains healthy bones and teeth; iron, which prevents anemia and strengthens the immune system; and copper, which keeps the cardiovascular system running. After sweet potatoes, raw carrots scored next, then collard greens, red peppers, kale, dandelion greens, spinach, and broccoli.

Its high concentration of carbohydrates and vitamin A and its relatively low water content make the sweet potato an excellent food source. It grows well under a wide range of farming conditions, including drought, pest infestation, and poor or water-logged soils. The nutritious sweet potato is inexpensive to produce and easy to cultivate; it has a short growing season and gives generally high yields.

Tomatillo

Tomatillos look just like little green tomatoes with paper wrappers on. These little fruits, relatives of tomatoes, have been cultivated since the time of the Aztecs. They have a tart and tangy flavor and are usually used in salsa, sauces, and stews. Unlike red tomatoes, tomatillos are usually never eaten raw. While they can ripen to yellow, tomatillos are generally used while they are green and firm—and always unwrapped.

Tomato

Tomatoes were being grown in the river valleys of coastal Peru from the dawn of human settlement. It is thought that tomatoes were originally weeds in cornfields before they were brought under cultivation. The wild tomatoes grew no larger than berries—and they were green—but with careful cultivation, the yields were increased and new varieties developed. Tomato cultivation spread up through Central America to Mexico and thrived in pre-Maya gardens, where they were thought to be a staple thousands of years ago. Over the years, farmers bred for specific factors, including color, and developed varieties such as the highly prized yellow tomato. Tomatoes were used to season dishes and to make sauces; they provided a valuable addition of vitamins A and C to an essentially corn-based diet. By the sixteenth century, pre-Columbian farmers had developed large red tomatoes and yellow tomatoes, which were sold in the Aztec marketplaces.

Tomatoes were introduced to Europe in 1523, but were eaten only in Italy for the following two hundred years. In England, tomatoes were grown purely as ornamental plants during that time. Other Europeans thought that the fruit was poisonous and refused to eat it at all. Sixteenth-century cooks in Florence, however, served fried green tomatoes and frittatas of green tomatoes. Ripe tomatoes were avoided at first because of their reputed passion-provoking properties, the soft, supple skin of the ripe red tomato along with the fruit's sensual red color and its succulent round form, surely meant that the tomato was too sinful for the moral minded to eat. The first recipe for ripe red tomatoes reportedly appeared in the nineteenth century—this was a recipe for tomato sauce published in an Italian cookbook.

Today, of course, the tomato is the basis of many sauces and condiments, and it is perhaps the most popular produce item in the Western world.

Vanilla

Vanilla, called the "queen of flavorings," is a native of Mexico. A member of the orchid family, vanilla is an epiphyte, a plant that obtains its food and water from the air while it grows anchored to another plant. The vanilla plant produces beautiful lime-yellow orchid blossoms, which only last a day. These blossoms give way to a cluster of long, green pods: the prized vanilla bean. The Aztecs called vanilla *tlilxochitl* ("the black flower") and used it to flavor their cocoa-based drinks. They and earlier peoples who lived near the Gulf of Mexico cultivated and cured vanilla—an incredibly complex feat even by today's standards.

In nature, the vanilla flower can be pollinated by only one species of bee and one species of hummingbird. Without these pollinators, no fruit develops on the plant. Today, plants are cultivated and pollinated by hand using a wooden needle. After pollination, it takes nine or ten months for the bean to mature. The mature beans, however, do not have the flavor or fragrance associated with vanilla. The green beans must first be cured. The beans are boiled for twenty seconds to stop them from ripening, then they are alternately heated in the sun during the day and wrapped in blankets to sweat at night for the next three to six months—a process that causes the beans to ferment. The beans shrink down, turn dark brown, and develop that wonderful aromatic vanilla flavor gourmets so highly prize.

Wild Rice

Wild rice is known for its full-bodied nutty flavor, its chewy texture, and its hefty price tag. Highly prized by gourmets, especially in Europe, wild rice is really not a rice, but rather a long-grain marsh grass native to the Great Lakes area. When the grain is ready in late summer, Sioux and Chippewa Indians harvest the wild rice in the traditional way in two-man canoes.

Only Native Americans may harvest the wild rice grown on their reservations. Often it's a husband and wife team that will paddle out onto the lakes and streams to harvest the rice. The man, standing in the stern, will pole through the tall grass while the woman, sitting in the bow, bends the heads of the grass over the sides of the canoe using a wooden flail. As she pulls the grass into the canoe, the woman taps the heads lightly with a second flail, releasing the rice seeds into the canoe.

Until recently, wild rice was a scarce commodity in the world marketplace, but a variety developed in 1968 has made it possible to grow wild rice on a larger commercial scale and to harvest it more economically using machinery. This nutritious grain, high in protein, fiber, B vitamins, and minerals, is still grown only in North America, with 80 percent of the total crop coming from Minnesota.

NOTE

Wild rice is available in supermarkets and gourmet specialty stores. Because it's relatively scarce, it's expensive. But wild rice goes further than regular rice: One cup raw will yield three and a half cups cooked. It should be washed well before cooking. Wild rice has a nutty, earthy taste and a chewy texture; it combines well with mushrooms, onions, and chopped nuts. Serve wild rice with chicken or fish dishes, or—as the Chippewa do—with wild game.

TOUCANS

Dwelling in the rain forest canopy, toucans are boldly colored birds with patterns of red, yellow, black, orange, green, blue, or white plumage; but their most distinctive feature is their large beak. Toucan bills are huge—often exceeding the length of the bird's body—and are colored bright yellow, orange, or red. Besides being important for courtship display and mate recognition, toucans use their beaks to reach fruit that is far out on fragile twigs. Toucans also use their beaks to intimidate other birds who try to rob their nests, but the beaks are actually very light for their size and are of little use in defense against the toucan's chief enemies: weasels and hawks.

To eat, the toucan will hold a piece of fruit in the very tip of its beak, then deftly snap its head back, open its beak, and toss the morsel down its throat. After feeding on large fruits, the birds fly off, carrying the seeds away from the shadow of the parent trees. After digesting the fruit, the birds often drop the seeds in places where there is enough sunlight for them to germinate and grow; thus the toucan plays a major role in seed dispersal in the rain forest.

Gregarious and noisy, toucans move about in groups of twelve to fifty individuals. In the early morning and late afternoon their call, a sound resembling a squeaky wheel, can be heard throughout the forest. The birds nest in natural tree holes, which they expand by removing rotten wood. The nest holds two to four eggs, incubated by both the male and female toucans. The young toucans emerge from their eggs with no feathers and develop very slowly. After the young birds learn to fly, they return to roost with their parents, often staying for months before they go off on their own. Toucans are weak fliers; they generally glide short distances between trees. Unlike other birds, toucans move their tails up and down during flight. At night when they roost, their tails stand directly up, and the birds sleep with their huge beaks resting on their backs covered by their raised tails.

While toucans are often hunted for sport or to collect their colorful beaks, they also have a spiritual significance for tribal peoples.

COOKING BASICS

Dendrobates auratus

Fundamentals

Before discussing cooking methods and getting into specific recipes, we need to review the basic elements of really good, creative cooking: stocks and sauces. Often people complain, "I got this recipe from the chef himself, and I followed it exactly, but it doesn't taste the same." The reason probably lies in one of the key ingredients: the stock. Stock from a can or, worse, from a bouillon cube does not give the same results as stock produced from boiling bones in your own kitchen. Canned stock will be watery and give only a slight meat or fish flavor to your dish; the bouillon cube will add only a salty flavor—but a thick, homemade stock will give a rich, wonderful aroma and taste to your dishes that will elevate them way above ordinary. Now, it's true that you can use canned stock or bouillon cubes for stock in recipes, but your dishes will never taste like the ones you are trying to re-create. Here's a hint: A good restaurant always has a stock pot simmering on the stove. Refer back to these basic procedures when reading the following recipes. If you lay in a cache of stock and roux in your freezer, cooking will be a breeze; much of the work involved in cooking is in the making of these two basics—and here, too, is the source of a lot of the flavor and quality!

Rich Chicken Stock

Makes 1 quart

While it does require a day on your stove to fully cook, this stock is easy to make. The resulting thick, gelatinous stock can be refrigerated for weeks or frozen indefinitely—so you can make it ahead. In fact, you can make enough to supply your cooking needs for several months in just one day. Stock is low in calories and high in protein. You can use it to make soups and casseroles and to create sauces for meat and seafood dishes. While there are many versions and varieties of stocks, this one will allow you to work magic in your kitchen. Just 1 heaping tablespoon of this rich stock is equivalent to 1 cup of liquid stock.

$\frac{1}{2}$ pound carrots

$\frac{1}{2}$ stalk celery

2 medium onions

2 heads of garlic sliced in half (don't peel)

$\frac{3}{4}$ cup chopped fresh parsley

3 bay leaves

1 pinch dried thyme

10 peppercorns

5 pounds chicken bones and trimmings

Place all the ingredients, in the order given, in a large stock pot; don't bother to chop the vegetables. Add cold water to cover. Cook, covered, over low heat, for 8 hours. Never boil the stock or it will become cloudy.

Place a large sieve over another large stock pot; carefully strain the liquid. Reserve the liquid; discard the solids. Strain the liquid a second time through a cheesecloth-lined sieve; reserve the liquid and discard the solids. At this stage, there will be about 3 gallons of stock.

Let the liquid stand in the refrigerator until the fat accumulates on top, 1 to 2 hours; carefully skim off the fat. The stock should have the consistency of a soft gelatin. Place the stock in a clean pot; cover and bring to a boil over high heat (it's okay to let the stock boil now because there's no fat). When the stock boils, remove the lid, reduce the heat to medium and simmer until the liquid is reduced to 1 quart, about 2 hours.

Remove the pot from the stove. Let the stock cool completely before storing. Pour the stock into small freezer containers; freeze indefinitely or refrigerate up to two weeks.

When reducing large quantities of liquid, such as 3 gallons of stock, it is important to ventilate your kitchen. Either use your stove fan or open the windows, otherwise you will create a mini-steambath in your house; the steam will condense on your walls and windows, and the aroma of whatever you are reducing will permeate the air as well as your furnishings. This caveat extends to long-term simmering of beans, soups, stews, and sauces.

Roux

Makes about 1 1/2 cups

Another basic element of many soups and sauces is called a roux. A roux is simply flour that has been cooked with oil to a varying degree of brownness. It's used as a thickener for sauces and soups. Although roux is made of flour, please don't think that using flour as a thickener will give you the same results. The secret lies in the fact that the roux is cooked separately, and the combination of heat and oil gives the flour a wonderfully nutty full flavor that carries over into your soups and sauces.

To make a roux, you use equal parts of oil and flour, making this recipe easy to adjust for any desired quantity. We prefer to use peanut oil in our roux, but any good vegetable oil would be fine in this recipe. Roux can be made ahead and stored; it will keep for several weeks in a covered jar in your refrigerator, or you can freeze it.

1 cup peanut oil
1 cup all-purpose flour

Using Roux as a Thickener

When using a roux to thicken sauces or soups, always add the liquid to the roux, not the roux to the liquid. Slowly add the liquid to the roux, whisking constantly until thoroughly combined (both ingredients should be at room temperature). Place the mixture over medium heat and cook, stirring constantly, until thick.

Heat the oil in a heavy pot or cast-iron skillet. When the oil is hot, remove the pot from the heat. Add the flour; using a whisk, mix the flour and oil thoroughly. Return the pot to the heat; cook over low heat, stirring often, until the flour is brown and gives off a nutty smell, about 6 to 8 minutes; do not let the mixture burn. Remove the mixture from the heat and store in an airtight container. Bring to room temperature before using.

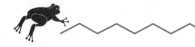

Crème Fraîche

Makes about 1 cup

This is a culture of heavy cream with buttermilk. Variations of the basic French recipe are produced throughout Latin America. Because you are working with a live culture, it's very important that you use sanitary utensils and containers. If you don't want to make your own, you can substitute sour cream, but you won't create the same taste.

1 cup heavy cream
1 tablespoon buttermilk

Mix the cream and buttermilk in a medium-size bowl; place the mixture into a sanitary plastic container. Cover with cheesecloth or a napkin (do not use a plastic lid, because the mixture must be able to breathe) and leave it for 2 days at room temperature. Mix well; refrigerate to stabilize the sauce in a bowl covered with a plastic lid.

Crème Fraîche will keep well in the refrigerator for 1½ to 2 weeks. Use it to top beans, rice, tacos, or enchiladas; to finish sauces; or, with a little sweetening, to top desserts or fresh fruits.

NOTE

If you don't have a deep-frying thermometer, you should consider buying one; it's a good kitchen tool. A candy thermometer, however, is even more versatile, and you'll find that it comes in handy for different types of cooking.

Clean Versus Sanitary

Clean generally means neat and dirt free (for example, clean shoes and a clean floor), whereas *sanitary* specifically means sterile or disinfected (that is, germ and bacteria free). Just because something is clean does not mean that it is also sanitary. Since crème fraîche contains a live culture, it is very important that there are no competing bacteria in unseen residue on the container. Uninvited bacteria can cause off-flavors and food-borne illnesses. Before making crème fraîche, it is wise to pour boiling water over the containers and utensils to make sure they are sanitary.

COOKING METHODS EXPLAINED

Frying

When frying, always remember to start with clean oil; don't reuse oil. Peanut oil and polyunsaturated oils, such as sunflower oil, are good for frying. If you are using a frying pan instead of a deep fryer, don't fill the pan higher than halfway up the side with oil. The secret of nongreasy frying is always to maintain the proper temperature in the pan: between 350 and 375°F. Heat the oil to the proper temperature before you start cooking—never put the food in the oil before it is sufficiently hot or the food will be greasy and soggy. The oil should be hot enough to form a seal around the food the minute it hits the pan; this will lock in the moisture and seal out the grease.

Tips for Frying

- Make sure the oil has reached the proper frying temperature before adding food to the pan. Then, allow the temperature to rise again to the proper temperature before adding more food.

- Don't crowd the frying pan; cook your food in two or more batches if necessary.

- Never let the oil smoke or burn. If the oil gets too hot and begins to smoke, immediately reduce the heat or remove the pan from the heat to cool down the oil. If allowed to become too hot, the oil will turn brown and develop an off-flavor.

- When frying chicken in a pan, make sure you have enough oil to cover at least half the thickness of the pieces.

- When frying fish, it's best to use a breading or batter. This prevents the fish fillet or steak from falling apart while cooking.

- Placing a screen or grate over your frying pan will keep the grease from splattering while allowing the steam to escape.

Sautéing

Sautéing means to cook small portions of food rapidly over high heat, using a minimum amount of oil. As a general guide, use 1 tablespoon for a 10-inch skillet or 2 tablespoons for a large pot or pan. When sautéing, not all the food is being touched by the hot oil, so it is important that the pieces of food be flat and of uniform thickness or else they will not cook evenly. When you have finished sautéing, deglaze the pan. Pour about ½ cup of wine or fruit juice (such as apple or mango) into the pan and loosen up the browned bits and the concentrated flavors left in the bottom of the pan. Pour the juices over the cooked food before serving.

Tips for Sautéing

- Heat the oil to 350°F before adding the food.

- After adding food to the pan, make sure the oil has returned to the proper temperature before adding more.

- Don't crowd the frying pan; cook your food in two or more batches if you have to.

- Never let the oil smoke or burn. If the oil gets too hot and begins to smoke, immediately reduce the heat or remove the pan from the heat to cool down the oil. If allowed to become too hot, the oil will turn brown and develop an off-flavor.

- Always keep the oil clean; wipe the pan out and add fresh oil before starting another batch.

- When sautéing meat, turn it over when the top begins to sweat.

Roasting

Meats and poultry come out better when roasted in an oven cooking bag; the bag holds the juices; and works like a smoker, allowing the steam to penetrate the meat so that it retains its moisture as it cooks. (And because the bags are disposable, there's little cleanup!) Always start with a preheated 400°F oven. Put the meat and any seasoning or condiments into the bag, tie the bag, and place the contents into a roasting pan with at least 2-inch sides. Prick five or six little vents in the bag with a knife tip. Insert a meat thermometer through the bag and into the meat so its tip is in the center of the thickest part of the meat and does not touch fat or bone. Place the prepared meat in the oven. When the outside begins to brown, in 15 to 20 minutes, turn the oven down to 350°F for meat and 280°F for poultry. Roast the meat slowly until the thermometer reaches 180°F. If you aren't using a cooking bag, roast chicken and turkey at a minimum of 325°F.

Another great—but entirely different—method of roasting is just "for the birds." It produces a chicken with crisp, nutty-flavored skin and moist flavorful meat. Wash, rinse, dry, and then salt the bird. Place garlic or herbs, if desired, in the cavity under the skin. Place the chicken in a shallow roasting pan (this time without an oven cooking bag). For a 3½-pound bird, cook the chicken, breast side down, in a preheated 475°F oven for 15 minutes, then turn the chicken breast side up, and continue to roast until done, about 40 minutes.

Barbecuing

Never put barbecue sauce on the meat before you start to cooking it. Most barbecue sauces have a high concentration of sugar, which will burn before your meat is thoroughly cooked. Marinate the meat first; then while barbecuing, baste the meat with the marinade. If the marinade has no oil in it, put it in a squirt bottle for a more creative approach to basting. When the meat is almost done, brush on the barbecue sauce. The meat will be flavorful and moist, and the sauce will add a great color and taste. Fish such as tuna and salmon, whose natural flavors are enhanced by the smoky flavor of the barbecue, should be basted often with an oil-based marinade to prevent sticking, since fish have little fat of their own.

Tips for Grilling

- Even cooking temperature is key to successful grilling.

- Before you start to grill, let the coals burn down to an ashy gray color, so that they'll give off a nice, white hot, even heat. Coals should not be red hot. It usually takes about 30 minutes for coals to reach this stage, so plan accordingly and don't rush.

- Gas grills have gauges: set the gauge to medium (350°F to 375°F) and allow the grill to reach that temperature before cooking. Placing food on a grill which has not been adequately preheated will cause the meats to stick, cook unevenly, and have all-around unpleasant results.

Broiling

When broiling, make sure the meat is not too close to the heating element; 2½ to 3 inches is close enough. Put the meat on a perforated double pan with some water in the bottom so that the fat and the meat juices will drip down into the water bath below. Instead of water, you can use wine or fruit juice (such as apple or mango). Try adding fresh herbs or spices to the liquid; the heat will cause the steam from the spiced liquid to rise up and infuse the meat with extra flavor.

Cooking Vegetables

The best way to cook green vegetables is to blanch them first. To blanch vegetables, bring water to a boil (use a ratio of two parts water to one part vegetable), add 2 tablespoons of fresh lemon juice or white vinegar (to hold the vegetable's color), and toss in the vegetables. Bring the water back to a boil; then immediately remove the vegetables and plunge them into cold water to stop the cooking process. Store the blanched vegetables in the refrigerator until you are ready to use them. Serve the vegetables cold, as finger foods or in salads. Or warm them in the microwave; sauté them; or add them to soups, stews, or casseroles. Blanching removes little of the vitamins and minerals and leaves the vegetables with a nice crunch.

Guide to Cooking Times for Fish

Because the density, texture, fat content, and moisture content vary from fish to fish, each species has a different ideal cooking time. You want the cooked fish to be firm but still juicy. You never want to cook the fish until it flakes (the old standard of doneness), because by then the fish will be tough and dry.

To determine the perfect cooking time, lay the fish (whether it's a steak, fillet, or whole fish) flat on a cutting board and measure it at its thickest part. For each inch, use the following cooking times as a rough guide; divide the total time in half to get the cooking time per side (6 minutes equals 3 minutes per side).

6 Minutes

Sand dab
Sole
Tilapia
Tuna

8 Minutes

Halibut
Swordfish

9 Minutes

Salmon
Shark
Trout

10 Minutes

Catfish
Mahi mahi
Rockfish (Pacific snapper)

12 Minutes

Monkfish
White sea bass

These cooking guidelines are based on those developed by the National Fish and Seafood Promotional Council. The council stresses that the important thing when cooking your fish is that you cook it just until it is firm but still juicy and has just turned from translucent to opaque. Remember, undercooked fish is preferable to overcooked fish.

The Perfect Meal

El Cocodrilo complements its dishes with servings of fresh vegetables; rice, potatoes, or other grains; black beans; and fresh salsas. By using fresh seasonal varieties at the peak of their ripeness, we are able to meet our goal of creating visual pleasure, gustatory satisfaction, and nutritional balance on each plate. These are factors that you, too, should consider when planning your meals.

Visual Pleasure

You should present on the plate an appetizing composition that includes a pleasing contrast of colors and textures.

Gustatory Satisfaction

You should present a dish with contrasting and complementary aromas and tastes (for example hot, spicy, mild, and sweet) that stimulate and please the palate.

Nutritional Balance

You should prepare a meal that includes green and yellow vegetables, complex carbohydrates (for example, rice and whole grains), and protein.

The *art* of cooking is simply to coordinate these factors to produce a meal that is satisfying on all three levels. In other words, it should look good, taste good, and be good for you!

PLEASE NOTE

Most of the recipes serve four, which makes it easy for you to divide them in half to serve two or to double them to serve eight. The recipes for salsas, sauces, compound butters, and spice mixtures will often make more than you will need for one meal or one recipe. Because these mixtures store well, you'll have them on hand to create many other great dishes with little further effort on your part.

When buying fish steaks or fillets, allow 6 ounces per person. When preparing recipes for fish, refer to "Cooking Methods Explained" (page 41) and "Guide to Cooking Times for Fish" (page 43).

When cooking a whole chicken, allow 1 pound per person; if the chicken is boneless, allow 8 ounces per person. When cooking beef, lamb, or pork, allow 8 to 10 ounces per person. When preparing recipes with chicken or meat, please refer to "Cooking Methods Explained" (pages 41) for tips on improving or varying your cooking techniques.

The recipes in this book generally call for the meat or fish to be sautéed, because sautéing is the easiest, tastiest method for cooking all types of fish and for meat and poultry in general. Plus the results are predictably wonderful. However, don't be afraid to try a recipe using a different cooking method; for example, you might want to roast a chicken instead of sautéing it. The salsas and sauces from one dish can often be used in another dish to create new and delicious flavor combinations. Experiment!

A few of the ingredients used in this book may seem exotic; however, they are becoming increasingly common on supermarket shelves, especially in cities or areas that have a mixture of ethnic populations. Sidebars, notes, and footnotes referred to throughout the book offer suggestions for substitutions of some uncommon ingredients. If you have trouble finding an ingredient in your local supermarket, try looking in natural food stores, gourmet food shops, and Latin American or Asian specialty markets. The Crocodile's Bodega, El Cocodrilo's mail order source for Latin American spices, condiments, and groceries, can supply you with Habanero Hot Sauce, Jamaican Jerk Seasoning, Cajun Blacken-

ing Spices, Ibarra Mexican Chocolate, Achiote Paste, Japanese Bread Crumbs, Chipotle Chile in Adobo, Masa Harina, Brazil Nuts, Quinoa, etc. (For a catalog: phone or fax 408-375-7108, or e-mail: cocofish@cocofish.com). Mail Order (page 153) lists establishments that can supply you with the specialty foods, chiles, or fresh produce needed for recipes in this book.

And—if you have any questions about ingredients or recipes used in this book, or about cooking with *El Cocodrilo's Cookbook*— just ask Chef Julio:

e-mail : cocofish@cocofish.com

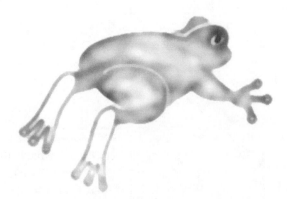

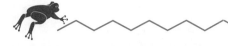

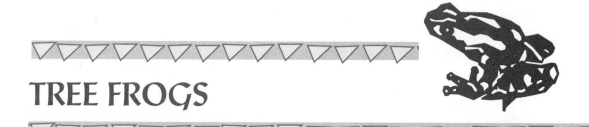

TREE FROGS

ree frogs are the jewels of the rain forest: vivid reds, blues, greens, and yellows contrast with black in striking patterns on their skins. These frogs are small—some are so tiny that they measure only one-half inch in total length. Sticky adhesive pads at the ends of their fingers and toes help the frogs move about and even cling vertically to the leaves and branches of the trees as they hunt for insects. Strong hind leg muscles rocket the frogs into the air at the first hint of danger or at the first sight of an insect meal, and they propel swimming frogs quickly through the water. Sticky tongues enable tree frogs to snatch insects from the air.

In the evening, tree frogs provide the night music for the rain forest. Groups of males compete in a loud chorus to attract mates. Females lack vocal sacs and are usually silent.

After mating, some frogs carry their eggs around in "backpacks." These skinfolds on the backs of some species form completely enclosed pouches in which the eggs develop. Other species build mud nests and stand guard over their clutches, catching any insects that threaten their eggs. Some species of tree frogs deposit their eggs on leaves that hang over rivers, lakes, or ponds; when the tadpoles hatch, they simply fall into the water below. Some species of ground-dwelling tree frogs lay their eggs in the damp forest floor. When the tadpoles hatch, one of the parent frogs returns, and the tadpoles squirm onto their parent's back for a piggyback ride. The adult frog will carry the tadpoles until they are ready to fend for themselves.

One species of dart-poison frog, known in the Amazon as kokoe'-pa', provides the most extreme example of parental devotion among frogs. They are ground-dwelling tree frogs, but after their eggs have hatched, the females climb high into the trees, carrying their offspring on their backs. They deposit their young, one by one, into the protective pools of individual bromeliads.

Bromeliads are funnel-shaped plants that have a rosette of stiff, narrow leaves that form a basin in the center of the plant where rainwater collects. While bromeliads vary in size, the reservoirs of some of the larger bromeliads can hold over a gallon of water. Native only to the American tropics, these plants grow on other plants high above the forest floor where they festoon the trees by the thousands.

The kokoe'-pa' females do not abandon their offspring in the bromeliads. They will later climb back up the same trees and visit each plant. On the second trip, the females deposit nonfertile eggs in each of the bromeliad pools so that the developing froglets will be sure to have something nutritious to eat.

Some tree frogs spend their whole lives in bromeliads. Besides rainwater, organic material also collects in the plant's central pool. This provides fertilizer for the plants and food for other tiny animals. Some species of tree frogs lay their eggs directly in these pools. There, the tiny tadpoles hatch and feed on the bacteria and algae in the water. The water in the pool keeps the frog's skin moist, and it also attracts insects for the adult frog's dinner. Some frogs hatch, grow up, and die in one single bromeliad plant, sharing this home with spiders, crabs, and lizards—a tiny world in a plant.

Dart-poison (or arrow-poison) frogs are probably the most famous tree frogs. These brilliantly colored frogs often match the bright-colored tropical foliage around them. Although insects may be attracted to the edible leaves, predators such as bats, rats, snakes, hawks, and large fish will steer clear of these frogs, because their neon coloration warns that they are deadly. Glands in the skins of these frogs produce a bitter-tasting poison, toxic to predators.

The dart-poison frog family contains more than 120 species that live mainly in the rain forests from Nicaragua to southeastern Brazil and Bolivia. Tribal peoples hunt the exceptionally poisonous species of frogs, then roast them to secrete their poisons. Hunters treat the tips of their blowgun darts with the collected frog poison; they can coat fifteen darts with the poison of just one frog. A single dart can paralyze a bird or a small monkey, which the tribe hunts for food.

The poison that the frog produces is actually an anesthetic that is 160,000 times more powerful than cocaine. Known as tetrodotoxin, this substance is used in Western medicine as a painkiller, anesthetic, and muscle relaxant. Tetrodotoxin is also used by voodoo doctors in Haiti to induce trances and create zombies.

Frogs have been around for more than two hundred million years. They are an important link in the global food chain. Like many forest species, tree frogs are a rich source of potentially beneficial chemicals. Because frogs eat low on the food chain, they also serve as early warning indicators of problems in the environment. In several areas of the planet, whole species of frogs have disappeared; in Costa Rica the golden toad has not been seen for years. Serious attention must be paid to the changes that are happening in the habitats of these creatures, because what affects them, ultimately, will affect humankind.

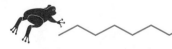

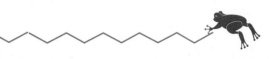

SALSAS, SAUCES, AND CONDIMENTS

Tᴀᴘɪʀᴜꜱ ʙᴀɪʀᴅɪɪ

sing a variety of herbs, spices, seeds, and nuts in the recipes adds another dimension of flavor to the dishes. Combining seasonal fruits and vegetables into fresh salsas not only stimulates the taste buds but adds complexity, color, and nutritional value to the dish.

CHILE PEPPERS

Chile peppers are one of our favorite seasoning ingredients. Chiles come in dozens of varieties, each one with its own particular taste and degree of hotness. We often use serranos, jalapeños, pequins, habaneros, arboles, or pasillas in our recipes. Please don't be afraid to season with peppers: When used in proper proportions, chiles will contribute a lot of flavor and zest to your dishes (as well as a good amount of vitamin C) without overwhelming the other ingredients.

Roasting Peppers

Gas range method: You can easily roast a small quantity of peppers by holding the peppers over the flame using a fork or tongs or place them on a wire screen directly over a burner. Roast each pepper, turning frequently, until the skin is charred on all sides, 3 to 4 minutes. Transfer the peppers to a bowl; let them cool. Peel, seed, and devein the peppers under cold running water.

Oven method: For a large number of peppers, use an oven. Preheat the oven to 450°F. Spray the peppers with nonstick cooking spray, and place them on a baking sheet. Bake the peppers until skins begin to blister, about 45 minutes. Remove from the oven, place them in a plastic bag, and seal it. Set the bag aside for 10 minutes to allow the chiles to sweat—they will now peel easily. Peel, seed, and devein the peppers under cold running water.

Caution: Never touch your eyes after chopping a chile without washing your hands first!

Salsa Brava

Makes about 6 cups

This salsa is a sort of Caribbean coleslaw. It's a wonderful accompaniment to any spicy meal, and it's low calorie, flavorful, and nutritious! It will keep for a good week in the refrigerator, so it's a great make-ahead dish. Adjust the number of chiles to your taste, giving it just the right amount of kick.

2 medium carrots, julienned

½ small head white cabbage, shredded

½ medium onion, diced

½ green bell pepper, diced

½ red bell pepper, diced

4 serrano or jalapeño chiles, finely chopped

1½ teaspoons salt

½ teaspoon freshly ground black pepper

1 cup white vinegar

½ tablespoon sugar

Combine the carrots, cabbage, onion, green and red bell peppers, chiles, salt, and black pepper in a large bowl. Stir in the vinegar and sugar. Pack the salsa in an airtight nonreactive container and refrigerate for at least 8 hours before serving to allow the cabbage to pickle.

Putting Out the Flames!

The capsaicin in chile will not stop burning if you drink water; this will only spread the capsaicin—and the pain—around in your mouth. Instead, drink something basic like milk to neutralize the chile's bite or eat dairy products or starches such as rice, bread, or potatoes. Alcohol, such as beer or wine, is also effective, as it dissolves the capsaicin.

Calypso Salsa

Makes about 3½ cups

This salsa is tangy and fruity, with the flavor of pineapple and ginger. It's great with fish, chicken, and pasta dishes; or pour it on grilled pork chops.

1 cup diced pineapple

1 cup diced orange sections

½ cup diced jícama

¼ cup diced red onion

½ cup diced red bell pepper

1 serrano or jalapeño chile, minced

1 tablespoon freshly squeezed lime juice

½ teaspoon minced ginger root

1 tablespoon minced fresh mint

1 tablespoon passionfruit glaze (page 150) or honey

Combine all of the ingredients in a medium-size, nonreactive bowl. Cover and refrigerate, allowing the flavors to marry a few hours before serving.

Salsa Fresca

Makes about 6 cups

Use this flavorful and colorful salsa to garnish meat, egg, and seafood dishes. It's also great as a dip for tortilla chips.

- 1½ cups diced jícama
- 1 cup diced red onion
- 3 cups diced tomatoes
- 3 serrano or jalapeño chiles, minced
- 5 tablespoons chopped fresh cilantro
- ¼ cup freshly squeezed lemon juice
- 1 teaspoon salt
- ½ teaspoon freshly ground black pepper

Combine all of the ingredients in a nonreactive medium-size bowl; mix well. Adjust the salt and pepper to taste. Serve immediately or cover and refrigerate until ready to use.

NOTE

Use only fresh chiles in the salsa recipes. Do not use canned or pickled chiles such as jalapeños; you will be very disappointed with the results. Only fresh chiles will do—except for when the recipe calls for chipotles in adobo, which are canned.

Mango Salsa

Makes about 3 cups

- 1½ cups diced mangos (ripe but firm)
- ½ cup diced jícama
- ½ cup diced red bell pepper
- ½ to 2 serrano or jalapeño chiles, finely diced
- ½ cup diced, seeded, and drained tomatoes
- 2 tablespoons chopped fresh cilantro
- 2 tablespoons freshly squeezed orange juice
- 1 tablespoon freshly squeezed lime juice
- Salt and freshly ground black pepper to taste

Combine all of the ingredients in a nonreactive, medium-size bowl; mix well. Adjust the salt and pepper to taste. Cover and refrigerate at least 4 hours before serving.

Sun-Dried Cranberry Salsa

Makes about 3 cups

This salsa is a tasty accompaniment to fowl, pork, and enchiladas—and it's dynamite on salmon.

- 1½ cups diced tomatoes
- ¾ cup diced jícama
- ¼ cup diced red bell pepper
- ¼ cup diced red onion
- ¼ habanero chile*, minced
- 4 tablespoons sun-dried cranberries
- 2 tablespoons chopped fresh cilantro
- 2½ tablespoons freshly squeezed lime juice
- ¼ teaspoon freshly ground black pepper
- 1 teaspoon salt

Combine all of the ingredients in a medium-size, nonreactive bowl. Let the salsa stand 30 minutes at room temperature to allow the flavors to marry before serving. Serve at room temperature. Cover and refrigerate any remaining salsa.

Freshly Squeezed Citrus Juices

There is no substitute for the freshly squeezed lemon and lime juices called for in the recipes in this book. Bottled lemon and lime preparations, especially, will not give desirable results.

---

*Available in some supermarkets and in Latin markets. If necessary, substitute 2 fresh jalapeño chiles for each habanero.

Cranberry Citrus Salsa

Makes about 4 cups

You can serve this salsa well chilled or hot. It is great on duck, pork, chicken, and fish. Try it mixed with rice. Because this salsa is especially good with turkey, serve it next Thanksgiving to add a little kick to your holiday bird.

- 2 cups fresh or frozen cranberries
- 1 cup chopped yellow or red onions
- ½ cup freshly squeezed orange juice
- Zest from 1 orange, grated**
- 1 jalapeño chile, seeded and chopped
- ½ teaspoon minced fresh ginger
- 2 tablespoons + 2 teaspoons firmly packed light brown sugar
- 1 teaspoon honey
- 1½ tablespoons rice vinegar
- ½ to 1 tablespoon hot red pepper sauce
- 2 tablespoons chopped fresh cilantro

Combine all the ingredients in a medium saucepan; cook over high heat until the liquid comes to a boil. Remove from the heat; cool, stirring occasionally, making sure not to split the cranberries. Refrigerate covered in an airtight container until ready to use.

**The zest of the orange is the outermost peel of the fruit without any of the pith (white membrane). To remove the zest, use a zester or the fine side of a vegetable grater.

Pico de Gallo

Makes about 4 cups

This is a pickled mixture of fresh minced onions, chiles, and other vegetables. This salsa will keep for weeks, and it's a great condiment for rice, omelets, salads, seafood, and chicken dishes as well as for traditional Latin dishes such as tamales, tacos, and enchiladas. Watch out, though, it's habit forming!

    1 pound onions, minced and rinsed in
      cold water
    ¾ cup minced carrots, rinsed in cold
      water
    ¾ cup minced red bell pepper, rinsed
      in cold water
    5 habanero chiles* (page 150), minced
    1 cup rice vinegar
    1 cup white wine vinegar
    5 teaspoons sugar
    2½ teaspoons salt

Combine all of the ingredients in a large glass or plastic container with a lid. Cover and chill for 4 hours before serving.

---

*Available in some supermarkets and in Latin markets. If necessary, substitute 2 fresh jalapeño chiles for each habanero.

Chipotle Chile Butter

Makes about 2 cups

Use this lightly smoky, rich-flavored butter with its hint of chile to top grilled steaks or fish just before serving. Or use it for sautéing fresh vegetables, shrimp, or mushrooms—try it with portobello mushrooms for a really "meaty" vegetarian dish.

    1 tablespoon minced shallots
    1 teaspoon minced garlic
    3 chipotle chiles (canned smoked
      jalapeño chiles)
    ¼ cup chopped fresh cilantro
    ½ pound butter, at room temperature

Combine the shallots, garlic, chiles, and cilantro in a food processor. Process until smooth. Place the butter in a large bowl; using an electric mixer, whip the butter until it is stiff and white. Add the shallot mixture to the butter; mix until well combined. Cover and refrigerate in an airtight container until ready to use.

Roll Up the Butter!

You can roll any compound butter in plastic wrap and shape it into a tube. After it has been refrigerated, the butter will be hard, and you can then just slice off the amount you need. Better yet, freeze the butter, and it will keep for months.

Habanero-Peach Butter

Makes about 3 cups

This condiment is very low in sodium. The recipe makes enough butter to accompany several batches of Caribbean Spiced Mahi Mahi with Habanero-Peach Butter (page 118). The butter will keep well refrigerated—just slice off the appropriate amount as you need it. Try it on other dishes; it adds a light spicy and fruity flavor to chicken, pork, and seafood dishes.

- 2 tablespoons olive oil
- 2 habanero (page 150) or 4 jalapeño chiles, minced
- 1/2 medium red bell pepper, minced
- 1/2 medium shallot, minced
- 6 tablespoons balsamic vinegar*
- 1 tablespoon honey
- 3 large ripe peaches, unpeeled, pitted and sliced
- 3/4 pound unsalted butter, softened

Heat the oil over high heat in a medium saucepan. Add the chiles, bell pepper, and shallot; cook over high heat for 2 minutes. Add the vinegar and honey to the chile mixture, reduce the heat to low, and simmer until almost all the liquid has evaporated, about 3 minutes. Remove from the heat; cool.

Place 2 of the peaches and the butter in a food processor or blender. Process until well mixed. Add cooled chile mixture to the butter purée, and process until well blended. Transfer the butter mixture to small bowl.

Mince the remaining peach, add it to the butter mixture, and blend well. Cover and refrigerate in an airtight container until ready to use, or freeze it.

Roll Up the Butter!

You can roll any compound butter in plastic wrap and shape it into a tube. After it has been refrigerated, the butter will be hard, and you can then just slice off the amount you need. Better yet, freeze the butter, and it will keep for months.

---

*For this recipe, do not substitute another type of vinegar for the balsamic vinegar.

Roasted Habanero Butter

Makes 4 to 5 cups

This recipe can be easily halved to yield about 2 cups, but you'll enjoy it so much you'll just have to make more—sooner than you expect. Use this butter to sauté vegetables; to toss with simple pastas; or to top baked potatoes, fish, and grilled steaks. Try simply buttering your bread with it; it's delicious!

1 teaspoon peanut oil

2 habanero chiles (page 150), roasted*
   and minced

¼ cup diced onion

2 tablespoons minced garlic

1 pound butter, at room temperature

2 tablespoons tomato paste

2 tablespoons rice vinegar

2 tablespoons freshly squeezed lime juice

1 teaspoon salt

1 teaspoon sugar

6 green onions, finely chopped

2 tablespoons chopped fresh parsley

½ cup finely chopped Brazil nuts

½ cup Japanese** or other dried bread
   crumbs

Heat the oil in a 8-inch skillet. Cook the chiles, diced onion, and garlic over medium-high heat until golden brown, about 5 minutes. Remove from heat; cool.

Place the butter in a large bowl; using an electric mixer, whip it until it is stiff and white. Add the cooled vegetable mixture to the whipped butter; mix to combine. Add the tomato paste, vinegar, lime juice, salt, and sugar; mix until well combined. Add the green onions, parsley, nuts, and bread crumbs; mix well. Cover and refrigerate in an airtight container until ready to use, or freeze it.

*See "Roasting Peppers" on page 51.

**Japanese bread crumbs (*panko*) can be found with other bread crumbs and batter mixes in most supermarkets and are available through mail order.

Mango Butter

Makes 4 to 5 cups

If 4 or 5 cups of butter seems like too much to handle, you can easily halve this recipe to make about 2 cups. but once you try this you'll never go back to plain butter. Mango butter is excellent served on fish, calamari steaks, pasta, and vegetables. If you can't find passionfruit glaze, you can easily make your own.

- 1 pound butter, at room temperature
- 2 ripe mangos, peeled, pits removed and chopped (about 2 cups)
- 4 tablespoons passionfruit glaze or Apricot-Lime Glaze (page 150)
- 2 tablespoons freshly squeezed lime juice
- 1½ cups Japanese* or other dried bread crumbs
- 2 tablespoons minced fresh parsley

Place the butter in a large bowl; using an electric mixer, whip it until it is stiff and white. Set aside.

Place the mangos in a food processor or blender; purée. Add the mango purée, passionfruit glaze, lime juice, bread crumbs, and parsley to the butter. Mix well. Cover and refrigerate in an airtight container until ready to use, or freeze it.

---

*Japanese bread crumbs (*panko*) can be found with other bread crumbs and batter mixes in most supermarkets and are available through mail order.

Green Cashew Sauce

Makes about 2 cups

This flavorful mayonnaise gets it green color from the fresh cilantro. Besides adding a tangy twist to sandwiches, this sauce can be tossed with pasta for a great change from pesto. Serve the sauce with grilled tilapia or other fish: Place a spoonful of the sauce on a plate, spread it out, and place the cooked piece of fish on top. You may want to garnish the dish with Salsa Fresca (page 53).

- 1 cup roasted, salted cashews
- 2 garlic cloves, peeled
- 1 teaspoon chopped shallot
- 2 serrano chiles, chopped
- ¼ cup peanut oil
- 3 tablespoons rice vinegar
- 1 tablespoon water
- ⅔ cup chopped fresh cilantro
- Salt and freshly ground black pepper to taste

Place the cashews, garlic, shallot, and chiles in a food processor; process until the mixture forms a paste. With the food processor running, slowly add the oil in a thin, steady stream until the mixture is throughly combined. Add the vinegar, water, and cilantro, and process until the mixture becomes a smooth green paste. Season with salt and pepper. Serve immediately, or refrigerate— it will keep for up to 2 weeks.

Roasted Red Pepper Sauce

▽▽▽▽▽▽▽▽▽▽▽▽▽▽▽▽

Makes about 2 cups

Serve this sweet, colorful, and intensely flavorful sauce on Sweet Corn Tamales (page 73) or on any grilled or sautéed seafood dish.

- 3 roasted* red bell peppers
- 2 cups dry white wine
- 2 tablespoons minced shallots
- 1 teaspoon minced garlic
- 1/2 cup heavy cream
- 1/4 teaspoon ground red pepper
- 3/4 cup butter, softened
- 1/2 teaspoon salt

Place the bell peppers in a food processor; purée. Set aside.

Combine the wine, shallots, and garlic in a 12-inch skillet; cook over medium heat until the liquid reduces to 3 tablespoons, about 10 minutes. Reduce the heat; add the cream, 1 tablespoon at a time, to the wine mixture; stir well. Do not let the mixture boil. Add the ground red pepper, puréed bell peppers, and the butter to the wine mixture; mix well.

Place a medium-size sieve over a medium-size bowl. Strain the mixture, reserving the liquid; discard the solids. Add the salt, mixing well. Cover and refrigerate until ready to use.

Ground Red Pepper

Not to be confused with chili powder (a mixture of chile and spices used to make chili beans), ground red pepper (also called cayenne pepper) is ground, dried red chile peppers. It is readily available in the spice section of the supermarket.

Caiman Curry Sauce

▽▽▽▽▽▽▽▽▽▽▽▽▽▽▽▽

Makes about 5 cups

This aromatic, fruity, full-flavored sauce is great on catfish, snapper, and soft-shell crab.

- 1/4 cup peanut or vegetable oil
- 1/4 cup diced onion
- 1 teaspoon minced garlic
- Pinch of crushed red pepper flakes
- 1/4 cup all-purpose flour
- 3 cups water
- 4 cups unsweetened pineapple juice
- 2 tablespoons curry powder
- 1/2 cup raisins
- 1/2 cup shredded sweetened coconut
- 1 small ripe banana, chopped
- 1/2 cup chopped raw almonds
- 1/2 teaspoon salt
- 4 teaspoons sugar

Heat the oil in large saucepan; add the onion, garlic, and red pepper flakes. Cook over medium heat, stirring frequently, until the onion has softened, 3 to 5 minutes. Add the flour, a little at a time, stirring constantly until a paste forms. Slowly add the water and then the pineapple juice, stirring constantly to prevent lumps. Reduce the heat to low; add the curry powder, raisins, coconut, banana, almonds, salt, and sugar. Simmer until the mixture reduces by one-fourth, 10 to 12 minutes.

Transfer the mixture to a blender or food processor; purée. Place a medium-size sieve over a medium-size bowl. Strain the mixture, reserving the liquid; discard the solids. Cover and refrigerate until ready to use.

*See "Roasting Peppers" on page 51.

Papaya Curry Sauce

Makes about 6 cups

Even fruitier and smoother tasting than the Caiman Curry Sauce, this sauce is wonderful on fish or chicken breast fillets. Use it as a dip for fried shrimp or calamari.

> 4 cups Caiman Curry Sauce (page 59), cold
> One 1-pound papaya, pared and chopped (about 2 cups); seeds reserved

Combine the Caiman Curry Sauce and papaya in a food processor or blender; purée until smooth. Set aside.

Place a small sieve over a small bowl. Place the papaya seeds into the sieve; with the back of a spoon or by hand, push the seeds against the sieve to release their liquid. Add the liquid to the curry sauce; mix well. Refrigerate, covered, in an airtight container until ready to use. Heat gently before serving.

Roasted Garlic Sauce

Makes about 1½ cups

Try this sauce on pasta, chicken, roast pork, or any grilled or sautéed fish. It's particularly good on sautéed calamari steaks.

> 12 whole garlic cloves, roasted (see note on this page)
> 1 tablespoon peanut or vegetable oil
> 2 tablespoons chopped garlic
> 1 tablespoon all-purpose flour
> 1 cup heavy cream
> ½ cup milk
> 2 teaspoons chopped fresh parsley
> 2 teaspoons freshly squeezed lemon juice
> ½ teaspoon salt
> ¼ teaspoon freshly ground black pepper

Crush half of the roasted garlic cloves in a small bowl; set aside.

Heat the oil in a 10-inch skillet. Add the chopped garlic, and cook over medium-high heat, stirring frequently, until the garlic begins to brown, 3 to 5 minutes. Add the flour, a little at a time, stirring constantly, until a paste forms. Slowly add the cream, milk, and reserved crushed garlic, stirring constantly. Reduce the heat to low; simmer for 3 minutes. Add the parsley and lemon juice. Season with the salt and pepper. Garnish the dish with the remaining roasted garlic cloves.

To coat chicken or fish, measure the desired amount of Cajun Blackening Spices into a paper bag, add a piece of chicken or fish, and shake. Remove the coated piece, set aside, and shake up the next piece.

Cajun Blackening Spices

Makes about ½ cup

This recipe will make enough spicy coating for about 8 to 10 servings of meat or fish. You can double the recipe if you'd like; the mixture stores well. Adjust the degree of hotness by controlling the amount of ground red pepper you use. Remember, this seasoning is supposed to be spicy. Use it on pork, chicken, and fish. Grilling gives you a taste of the Louisiana bayous. When cooked over high heat, the Cajun spices caramelize and turn black, creating a unique flavor.

- 4 tablespoons sweet paprika
- 2 teaspoons ground red pepper
- 2 teaspoons salt
- 1 teaspoon white pepper
- 1 tablespoon onion powder
- 2 teaspoons garlic powder
- 2 teaspoons dried thyme
- 2 teaspoons dried oregano
- 2 teaspoons dried basil

Combine all of the ingredients in a small bowl; mix well. Store covered in an airtight container until ready to use.

Fresh Tomato Sauce

Makes about 4 cups

Perfect for egg dishes, pasta, and fresh fish, you can adjust the kick of this sauce with the habanero chile. Add more if you like it spicy.

- 1 red bell pepper, halved and seeded
- 4 garlic cloves, peeled
- 1 medium yellow onion, chopped
- 12 tomatoes (about 5 to 6 ounces each), peeled, halved, and seeded
- 2 teaspoons freshly ground black pepper
- 4 teaspoons salt
- 6 tablespoons rice vinegar
- 2½ teaspoons sugar
- ¼ habanero chile (page 150), minced

Preheat the oven to 350°F. Place the bell pepper, cut side down, the garlic, and the onion in a small baking dish. Roast until soft, about 30 minutes.

Combine the roasted vegetables, tomatoes, black pepper, salt, vinegar, sugar, and chile in a food processor; purée until smooth. Cover and refrigerate, up to one week, until ready to use.

Skinning a Tomato

Make small surface cuts into the tomato. Dip the tomato in boiling water for about 30 seconds. Remove with a slotted spoon and plunge into iced water. The skin will slip off easily.

Jamaican Jerk Spices

Jerk refers to the Caribbean method of preserving meats, fish, and poultry by using a dry or a wet rub of herbs and spices. Most of the recipes in this book use the dry rub, since the ingredients are easy to assemble and mix in large quantities. The dry rub will keep indefinitely. If you want to experiment, substitute the wet rub in any of the recipes.

Jamaican Jerk Spices—Dry

Makes about ½ cup

Use this very spicy, aromatic, and addictive mixture on barbecue, rub it on roasts, use it to make fajitas or sautéed vegetables. Experiment with it in different dishes—the sky's the limit!

- 2 teaspoons ground red pepper or 1 teaspoon ground habanero chile pepper (page 150)
- 2 tablespoons allspice
- 1 tablespoon ground nutmeg
- 4 teaspoons salt
- 4 teaspoons sugar
- 1 teaspoon freshly ground black pepper
- 2 tablespoons chopped dried onion
- 1½ teaspoons dried onion powder
- 2 tablespoons garlic powder
- 1½ teaspoons dried thyme
- 1½ teaspoons mustard seeds
- ⅛ teaspoon ground cloves
- 1½ teaspoons dried orange peel

Using a spice grinder or mortar and pestle, finely grind all of the ingredients. Store in a tightly sealed jar.

Jamaican Jerk Spices—Wet

Makes about 1 cup

Jerk seasoning imparts a taste of the West Indies to your meal. Rub this wet spice mixture inside the cavities of chicken, turkey, and split pork loins. Rub some more mixture on the outside, then barbecue, roast, or rotisserie the meat for a tasty treat. The chiles add the kick to this dish, so add as much as you like.

- 2 to 4 fresh habanero or 3 to 6 fresh jalapeño chiles, finely chopped
- ¼ cup ground allspice
- 1 tablespoon ground cinnamon
- 1 tablespoon ground nutmeg
- 2 teaspoons salt
- 1 tablespoon molasses
- 1 medium onion, chopped
- ¼ cup freshly squeezed lime juice
- 2 tablespoons chopped green onions
- 2 tablespoons grated orange zest*
- 1½ teaspoons tamarind paste, mango chutney, or molasses

Combine all of the ingredients in a food processor or blender; process or blend until well mixed and a paste forms. The mixture will keep in a sealed jar in the refrigerator for about one week.

> ## Be Careful!
>
> When making Jamaican Jerk Spices, be careful not to breathe in the spices or touch your eyes while you prepare this mixture.

---

*The zest of the orange is the outermost peel of the fruit without any of the pith (white membrane). To remove the zest, use a zester or the fine side of a vegetable grater.

Yucatecan Pibil Sauce

Makes about 7 cups

This flavorful sauce is our version of the classic Maya sauce so popular throughout the Yucatán Peninsula of Mexico. Use this rich, red sauce for braising chicken, pot roasts, ribs, and pork butts.

- 1 tablespoon peanut or vegetable oil
- 1¼ cups diced onions
- ¼ cup chopped garlic cloves
- ½ green bell pepper, chopped
- ½ red bell pepper, chopped
- ½ habanero chile (page 150), chopped
- 1 very ripe plantain, peeled and chopped
- 2½ tablespoons fresh chopped cilantro
- 3 sprigs fresh mint, chopped
- 1 cup Fresh Tomato Sauce (page 61)
- 1 (46-ounce) can unsweetened pineapple juice
- 2 tablespoons firmly packed dark brown sugar
- 3 ounces achiote paste (page 149)

Heat the oil in a 12-inch skillet. Add the onions, garlic, green and red bell peppers, chile, and plantain. Cook over low heat, stirring occasionally, until the ingredients begin to brown and become soft, 20 to 30 minutes. Add the cilantro, mint, Fresh Tomato Sauce, pineapple juice, brown sugar, and achiote paste. Stir well and simmer for 10 minutes. Remove from the heat.

Place the mixture in a food processor or blender; purée until smooth. Place a medium-size sieve over a medium-size bowl. Strain the sauce, reserving the liquid; discard the solids. If the sauce is too watery, return the mixture to the skillet and cook over medium heat until it reaches the desired consistency.

Plantains— The Cooking Banana

Plantains are also known as cooking bananas. Though native to Asia, plantains are extremely popular in Latin American and used extensively in everything from soups to desserts. When green, the plantain is used just as a potato would be in soups and stews; like a potato, it can be thinly sliced and pan fried. Tostones (page 81), thickly sliced and deep-fried plantains, are a finger food that can be eaten with a variety of salsas and often appear as a staple in Latin Caribbean meals. When the plantain is yellow with black spots, it is ripening but not yet sweet. A half black, half yellow plantain is ripe, and when it's baked with a little butter, brown sugar, and cinnamon, it makes a wonderful dessert. A black plantain is really ripe, sweet, and full-flavored. It can be used to flavor sauces and curries. In all cases, plantains must be cooked before eaten.

Criollo Marinade

▽▽▽▽▽▽▽▽▽▽▽▽▽▽▽

Makes about 2½ cups

This marinade has the wonderfully smoky flavor of achiote. Use it to marinate meats such as chicken, turkey, ribs, fish, and prawns; then barbecue, sauté, or grill as you wish.

- 1 cup soy sauce
- 1 cup peanut oil
- 1 tablespoon Cajun Blackening Spices (page 61)
- 2 teaspoons freshly ground black pepper
- 4 tablespoons achiote paste (page 149)
- 1 tablespoon minced garlic

Combine all of the ingredients in a large bowl; whisk until the oil and soy sauce are well blended. Store in a clean plastic container with a tight-fitting lid and refrigerate for up to 2 weeks.

Avocado Salsa

▽▽▽▽▽▽▽▽▽▽▽▽▽▽▽

Makes about 3 cups

This salsa is wonderful with Grilled Chicken Breast Criollo (page 121) or any blackened fish that is sautéed with Cajun Blackening Spices (page 61).

- 2 medium-size ripe Haas avocados, diced
- 1 tablespoon freshly squeezed lemon juice
- 1½ cups tomatoes, peeled*, seeded, and diced
- 2 serrano chiles, minced
- 3 tablespoons chopped green onions
- 3 tablespoons red wine vinegar
- 2 tablespoons olive oil
- 3 tablespoons chopped fresh cilantro
- Salt and freshly ground black pepper to taste

Combine the avocados and lemon juice in a medium-size bowl; mix gently. Add the remaining ingredients to the avocado mixture and mix gently together. Adjust the seasoning to taste. Cover and refrigerate 30 minutes to allow the flavors to marry.

*For how to peel a tomato, see page 61.

Wild Rice Salsa

Makes about 4½ cups

Try this salsa on salads and in chicken, fish, and meat dishes.

1 cup uncooked wild rice
¼ cup diced red bell pepper
1½ cups Salsa Fresca (page 53)
2 tablespoons chopped fresh cilantro
1 large chipotle chile (canned smoked jalapeño chile), minced
1 cup diced jícama
½ cup freshly squeezed lime juice
2 tablespoons olive oil
1½ tablespoons sugar
¼ teaspoon salt

Combine the rice and 4 cups of water in a medium saucepan; heat the mixture over medium heat just until it comes to a boil. Reduce the heat to low; simmer, covered, until the grains begin to open, 1 hour. Remove from the heat and drain. Spread the rice in a shallow pan and cool in the refrigerator, about 1 hour.

Combine the remaining ingredients in a nonreactive medium-size bowl, add the cooled rice, and mix well. Refrigerate covered in an airtight container for at least 8 hours to allow the flavors to marry. Store for up to 4 days.

Posole Salsa

Makes about 3 cups

This salsa is excellent in salads and fish, chicken, and meat dishes.

½ cup canned yellow hominy rinsed in cold water and well drained
½ cup canned white hominy, rinsed in cold water and well drained
⅓ cup diced red bell pepper
1 cup Salsa Fresca (page 53)
2 tablespoons chopped fresh cilantro
½ large chipotle chile (canned smoked jalapeño chile), minced
⅓ cup freshly squeezed lime juice
2 tablespoons olive oil
1 tablespoon sugar
⅛ teaspoon salt

Combine all of the ingredients in a medium-size plastic container with a tight-fitting lid; mix well. Refrigerate for 8 hours to let the flavors blend.

Red Hills Jerk Sauce

Makes about 1½ cups

Serve this sauce over rotisserie or roasted chicken, or paint it on the chicken as it roasts. This sauce is also wonderful on pork.

> ½ cup mango chutney
>
> ½ cup corn syrup
>
> 7 tablespoons cider vinegar
>
> 4 tablespoons Jamaican Jerk Spices—
>   Wet (page 62)
>
> 8 tablespoons molasses
>
> ½ cup water
>
> 1 teaspoon hot red pepper sauce

Combine the chutney, corn syrup, and 3 tablespoons of the vinegar in a food processor or blender; purée until smooth.

Combine the chutney mixture and remaining ingredients in a nonreactive small bowl; mix well. Refrigerate covered in an airtight container for up to 2 weeks.

Hold the Sauce!

If you must make the Yellow Pepper Beurre Blanc in advance, you can hold the sauce over a warm water bath for up to 2 hours.

Yellow Pepper Beurre Blanc

Makes about 1 cup

This is a quick and lovely sauce to make when yellow bell peppers are in season. Because the sauce must be used when it is ready—it will not keep in the refrigerator—make only the amount you will need for the meal at hand. Double the recipe if you are serving a large number of guests. Try this beurre blanc on everything—fish, pork, chicken, and even rice.

> 1½ yellow bell peppers, roasted*
>
> ¼ cup minced shallots
>
> ¼ cup dry white wine
>
> 1 cup butter, cut into 16 pieces
>
> ¼ teaspoon salt, or to taste
>
> 1 teaspoon sugar, or to taste

Place the roasted bell peppers in a food processor or blender; purée. Set aside.

Combine the shallots and wine in a 10-inch skillet; cook over medium heat until the liquid reduces down to one-fourth of the original amount. Reduce the heat to low; add the bell pepper purée, mixing well.

Add the butter to the vegetable mixture, one piece at a time, stirring constantly with a whisk, until well combined. (Do not allow the mixture to boil.) Season with the salt and sugar. Serve immediately.

*See "Roasting Peppers" on page 51.

Sweet Jalapeño Dipping Sauce

Makes about 1½ cups

Try this dipping sauce with Armadillo Eggs (page 77) or Sweet Potato Corn Cakes (page 78). Brush the sauce on a roasting chicken to get a tasty glaze. It also makes a great dipping sauce for whole fish.

- 1 cup unsweetened pineapple juice
- 2 jalapeño chiles, seeded and julienned
- 4 teaspoons honey
- ¼ cup sugar
- 2 tablespoons + 2 teaspoons freshly squeezed lime juice
- ¼ cup rice vinegar
- 2 tablespoons + 2 teaspoons red wine vinegar
- 2 tablespoons + 2 teaspoons freshly squeezed orange juice
- 1 heaping tablespoon grated orange zest*

Combine all of the ingredients in a medium saucepan; cook over medium heat until the mixture just comes to a boil. Reduce the heat to low and simmer 20 minutes. Remove from the heat; cool. Refrigerate covered in an airtight container for up to 2 weeks.

---

*The zest of the orange is the outermost peel of the fruit without any of the pith (white membrane). To remove the zest, use a zester or the fine side of a vegetable grater.

Sun-Dried Tomato and Serrano Chile Pesto

Makes about 4 cups

This pesto is excellent on steamed artichokes, fish, lamb, and steaks. Try it spread on French bread! Add more serrano chiles if you like it hot!

- ½ pound sun–dried tomatoes, not packed in oil
- 1 tablespoon rice vinegar
- 1 cup warm water
- 1 cup slivered or sliced almonds
- 5 tablespoons chopped fresh basil
- 2 tablespoons balsamic vinegar**
- 1 tablespoon minced serrano or jalapeño chiles
- ½ cup freshly grated Parmesan cheese
- ½ cup fresh or frozen thawed corn kernels
- ½ cup olive oil
- 1½ tablespoons hot red pepper sauce

Combine the tomatoes, rice vinegar, and water in a small nonreactive bowl. Let soak 1 hour; drain.

Add the almonds, basil, and tomato mixture to a food processor or blender; coarsely chop. Transfer the mixture to a large bowl. Mix in the remaining ingredients; combine thoroughly. Refrigerate covered in an airtight container up to 1 week.

**For this recipe, do not substitute another type of vinegar for the balsamic vinegar.

Cactus Pear Salsa

Makes about 4 cups

Serve this salsa chilled on roasted duck, pork, swordfish, shark, or salmon.

> 10 ripe, very red cactus pears, peeled
> Juice of 2 lemons
> 1/2 cup freshly squeezed orange juice
> 2 serrano or jalapeño chiles, minced
> 1 medium red onion, diced
> 1 green apple or pear, unpeeled, diced
> 1 tablespoon chopped fresh thyme
> 1/8 teaspoon ground cumin
> 1/8 teaspoon ground allspice
> 1 teaspoon sugar or honey
> Pinch of salt

Place 7 of the cactus pears and the lemon and orange juices in a medium saucepan; bring the liquid to a boil. Reduce the heat to low; simmer, covered, until the fruit is soft, about 10 minutes. Remove from the heat; set aside.

Place a medium-size sieve or food mill over a medium-size bowl. Push the sauce through the sieve with the back of a wooden spoon or process through the mill until only the seeds remain. Reserve the liquid; discard the solids.

Dice the remaining 3 cactus pears, and add them to the strained juice. Add the remaining ingredients to the cactus pear mixture; mix well. Refrigerate covered in an airtight container for up to 1 week.

Peeling a Cactus Pear

Peeling a cactus pear seems a little tricky, but it's actually easy. Even though the cactus pears sold commercially have been deprickled, tiny little hairs remain, which can be really annoying. To avoid pricking yourself, take a fork and push it into the side of the pear.

While holding the pear firmly with the fork, slice about 1/2 inch off the top and bottom ends with a sharp knife. Then make a slit in the skin that runs the length of the fruit; cut through the skin to the flesh, but don't cut through the flesh. Push the skin away from the fruit with the knife as you roll the fruit away from you with the fork. The skin will peel away, and you can then pick up the fruit with your hands.

TAPIRS

Tapirs live in the low light and high humidity of the rain forest's understory. They are the largest herbivores in the tropical American rain forest. They have long, moveable snouts—shorter versions of elephant trunks—which they use to pick up fallen fruit, strip leaves and buds from branches, or grasp branches and carry the leaves to their mouths. Using their snouts, tapirs stroke leaves until they find the ones that smell just right to eat. Waving these mini-trunks in the air, tapirs sniff for any scent of danger from their enemy, the jaguar. When in danger, tapirs are capable of running swiftly from their predators.

Tapirs travel alone or in pairs. Usually nocturnal, they trot along tunnel-like paths, which they have worn through the dense undergrowth of the forest floor. These paths may extend for miles. Tapirs spend much of their time in water or mud. The water cools them and allows them to get rid of pests—especially ticks. In the water, tapirs are excellent swimmers; there they dive to the bottom to root for swamp grass and water plants to eat. Like baby deer, tapirs are born with camouflage: Their little brown bodies are patterned with white stripes and spots that gradually fade as the animals grow into adulthood. The adult tapirs' coats are dark brownish gray, and the fur is short and thick, like woolen velvet.

While tapirs may look like large pigs (tropical American tapirs can grow to six hundred pounds) they are actually related to the horse and the rhinoceros. These shy, peaceful creatures have been roaming the earth for the last thirteen million years—and they've hardly changed at all. Their habitat, however, has shrunk and no longer includes Europe and North America.

APPETIZERS

CROCODYLUS ACUTUS

Pupusas

Salvadorian-style Stuffed Tortillas

Serves 6

The pupusa is a traditional "fast food" sold by street vendors in El Salvador. It's a thick, handmade tortilla stuffed with a savory filling and cooked to a golden brown. Other versions of pupusas, called by different names, are popular throughout Central America. Some favorite fillings include cheese, chicken, and pork skin cracklings. Serve with Salsa Brava (page 52).

3¾ cups masa harina (page 150)

2½ cups warm water

½ teaspoon freshly ground black pepper

1 teaspoon cumin

½ teaspoon hot red pepper sauce

1 green bell pepper, chopped

4 tomatoes, chopped

1 medium red onion, chopped

½ cup shredded mozzarella cheese

⅔ cup shredded, cooked chicken

2 tablespoons corn oil for cooking

Combine the masa harina and water in a medium-size bowl. Mix thoroughly until the dough just holds together; it will have the consistency of pie dough. Divide the dough into 12 balls: six 2-ounce balls and six 3-ounce balls. Set aside.

Place the black pepper, cumin, red pepper sauce, bell pepper, tomatoes, and onion in a food processor or blender; purée until well blended.

Flatten one 3-ounce ball of tortilla dough into a 5½- to 6½-inch circle. In the center of the tortilla, place 1 tablespoon of the puréed mixture, 1 tablespoon of the mozzarella cheese, and 2 tablespoons of the chicken.

Flatten one 2-ounce ball of tortilla dough into a 4- to 5-inch circle and place over the larger tortilla, covering the filling. Press the edges of both tortillas together, so they form a sealed pocket. Repeat this process five more times.

1. Flatten each ball of dough.

2. Place a smaller tortilla over the filling and seal the edges.

Pour 1 teaspoon of oil in a medium nonstick skillet and spread it around with a paper towel. Heat the oil; add 1 or 2 pupusas. Cook over medium heat, turning once, until golden brown on both sides, about 8 minutes. Repeat until all the pupusas are cooked.

Cheese Pupusas

Substitute 1¼ cups of shredded mozzarella cheese for both the chicken and the cheese in the pupusa filling. When filling the tortillas, top the purée mixture with 3 tablespoons of cheese. Continue as directed.

Sweet Corn Tamales

Serves 8

Serve these tamales unwrapped; topped with a tablespoon of Roasted Red Pepper Sauce (page 59); and accompanied by Black Beans Otomí (page 104), Crème Fraîche (page 40), or Salsa Fresca (page 53). Or you can eat them with your fingers just as they come out of the corn husk; they're irresistible!

 6 ears fresh corn, with husks
 ¾ cup cornmeal
 ¼ cup masa harina*
 1 to 3 teaspoons sugar, to taste
 ½ cup margarine
 1 teaspoon salt

Remove the husks from the corn; set husks aside.

With a knife, cut the corn kernels from the cobs. Place the kernels in a blender or food processor; purée. Add the corn purée, cornmeal, and masa harina to a medium-size bowl; mix well. Add the sugar, margarine, and salt to the corn mixture; mix thoroughly.

Place individual sections of corn husks onto a work surface; place 2 rounded tablespoons of the corn mixture in the middle of each section. Fold one side of the husk over the filling; then fold the other side on top and bring the bottom up to make a neat, secure "envelope" (the top will be open). Place folded husk on top of another corn husk, open side down. Repeat the folding pattern. You should have approximately 16 to 20 tamales when finished.

Layer the tamales, on their sides, in a stock pot. Cover the tamales with warm water, leaving the top layer exposed. Cook over low heat 1 hour and 15 minutes.

1. *Fold one side of the husk over the corn mixture.*

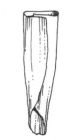

2. *Fold the other side of the husk on top.*

3. *Bring the bottom of the husk up to make a neat envelope (the top will be open).*

4. *Place the folded husk on top of another husk, open end down.*

---

*Masa harina and cornmeal are not the same thing. Masa harina is made from kernels of corn that have been soaked in lime, dried, and then specially ground. Masa is traditionally used to make tamales and tortillas; it is available in the flour section of many supermarkets and in Latin grocery stores.

5. *Repeat Steps 1 through 3.*

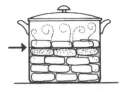

6. *Layer the tamales, on their sides, in a stock pot.*

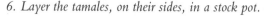

@   @   @

**Japanese bread crumbs (*panko*) can be found with other bread crumbs and batter mixes in most supermarkets and are available through mail order.

Jamaican Curry Crab Cakes

Serves 4 to 6

These make excellent appetizers, welcomed at any occasion. They're also great luncheon entrées. The distinctive curry flavor blends well with the taste of the crabmeat. Serve them with Caiman Curry Sauce (page 59), garnishing with Salsa Fresca (page 53).

2 cups (about 1 pound) crabmeat (rock or dungeness crab)
3 eggs
1/2 teaspoon salt
1/4 teaspoon hot red pepper sauce
1 teaspoon curry powder
1 tablespoon chopped fresh parsley
2 tablespoons melted butter
1/2 cup cashew nuts, finely chopped
1 cup Japanese** or other dried bread crumbs
Peanut oil for cooking

Place a medium-size colander into a medium-size bowl; add the crabmeat, and set aside.

Beat the eggs in a medium-size bowl; add the salt, red pepper sauce, curry powder, and parsley; mix well. Stir in the butter; set aside.

Squeeze the crabmeat to remove any excess water, and shred the meat with your fingers (be careful of shell fragments!). Add the crabmeat to the egg mixture; stir to combine. Add the nuts and bread crumbs; stir well. Cover and refrigerate 1 hour.

Shape the crab mixture into 12 patties. Heat about 1 tablespoon of the oil in a 12-inch skillet. Cook the patties over medium heat, turning once, until golden brown, about 7 minutes. Be careful not to overcrowd the pan; fry in batches if necessary. Serve immediately.

Flamingo Bay Shrimp Cakes with Brazil Nuts and Habanero Butter

Serves 4 or 8

This dish, which gets rave reviews, will serve 4 as a luncheon entrée or 8 as an appetizer.

½ pound calamari steak

3 eggs

1½ teaspoons salt

¾ teaspoon hot red pepper sauce

¼ teaspoon curry powder

1 stick (4 ounces) butter, melted

3 green onions, finely chopped

½ cup chopped Brazil nuts

1 pound rock shrimp, chopped

2½ cups Japanese* or other dried
   bread crumbs

Peanut oil, for cooking

4 tablespoons Roasted Habanero
   Butter (page 57)

½ cup heavy cream

4 tablespoons Salsa Fresca (page 53)

Place the calamari steak in a food processor or blender; purée until it forms a paste.

Combine the eggs, salt, red pepper sauce, curry powder, and melted butter in a large bowl. Mix in the calamari purée. Add the onions, Brazil nuts, and shrimp; stir well. Add the bread crumbs, a little at a time, mixing well after each addition.

Form the mixture into 16 patties. Heat about 1 tablespoon of oil in a 12-inch skillet. Cook the patties over medium heat, turning once, until brown and crispy, 8 to 9 minutes. Be careful not to overcrowd the pan; fry in batches if necessary.

While the patties are cooking, combine the Roasted Habanero Butter and cream in a small saucepan; cook over low heat just until butter melts and mixes with the cream. Spoon the warm sauce over the cooked patties, top with Salsa Fresca and serve immediately.

---

*Japanese bread crumbs (*panko*) can be found with other bread crumbs and batter mixes in most supermarkets and are available through mail order.

Flautas de Camarones

Shrimp Flutes

Serves 4

Flauta is the Spanish word for "flute," and these crunchy, golden-brown flutes—each stuffed with a shrimp—make great finger food for parties as well as favorite luncheon or dinner entrées. Be sure to cook them in several batches, so the oil remains at 350°F, or else the flautas will be soggy and greasy. Properly cooked, they'll be crispy on the outside and the shrimp will be juicy and tender within. Serve with Guacamole (page 83) and Green Cashew Sauce (page 58) or with Salsa Brava (page 52) and Crème Fraîche (page 40). Add a side of Black Beans Otomí (page 104), some rice, and a green salad, and you've got dinner!

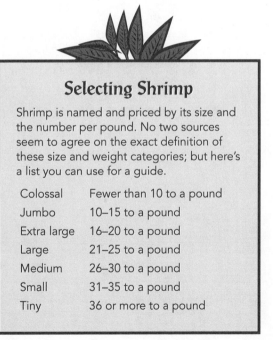

Selecting Shrimp

Shrimp is named and priced by its size and the number per pound. No two sources seem to agree on the exact definition of these size and weight categories; but here's a list you can use for a guide.

Colossal	Fewer than 10 to a pound
Jumbo	10–15 to a pound
Extra large	16–20 to a pound
Large	21–25 to a pound
Medium	26–30 to a pound
Small	31–35 to a pound
Tiny	36 or more to a pound

Peanut oil for frying
12 (4-inch) corn tortillas
12 extra-large shrimp, butterflied

Heat 2 inches of oil in a deep fryer or deep, heavy skillet, to 350°F. Using tongs, dip the tortillas, three or four at a time, into the oil until they have softened, 6 to 10 seconds. Drain on paper towels and cool.

Place 1 shrimp lengthwise near the bottom of one tortilla. Roll the shrimp in the tortilla and secure with a toothpick. Repeat to make 12 flautas.

Fry the flautas in the hot oil in several batches, until the tortilla is crispy and lightly golden, about 2 minutes.

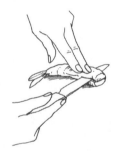

1. *Butterfly each shrimp.*

2. *Place 1 shrimp along the bottom of a tortilla.*

3. *Roll the shrimp in the tortilla and secure with a toothpick.*

Cilantro is also known as Chinese parsley. It's the fresh green leaves of the coriander plant; the dried seeds are ground to make the spice called coriander. Fresh cilantro is available in many supermarkets as well as in Asian and Latin markets.

Mussels in Cilantro and Serrano Cream Sauce

Serves 2

This dish looks as great as it tastes. The broth is especially tasty, so be sure to serve it with plenty of bread. Try varying the recipe with small clams such as manilas, cockles, littlenecks, or count necks. Garnish with Salsa Fresca if you want a little more color and tang.

1 teaspoon olive oil

2 tablespoons butter

2 teaspoons minced shallots

1 teaspoon minced garlic

12 mussels in their shells, scrubbed, cleaned, and debearded

$\frac{1}{2}$ cup dry white wine

$\frac{1}{4}$ cup heavy cream

1 tomato, diced

$\frac{1}{4}$ cup diced red onion

1 tablespoon chopped fresh cilantro

1 serrano or jalapeño chile, minced

Salsa Fresca (page 53), optional

Heat the oil and butter in a 12-inch skillet. Add the shallots, garlic, mussels, and wine, and cook over medium heat, covered, until the mussels open, about 3 minutes (discard any mussels that have not opened). Turn the heat to low, and simmer until the liquid has reduced by half, about 4 minutes. Add the cream, tomato, onion, cilantro, and chile; cook 2 minutes more.

To serve, arrange the mussels on a serving plate. Continue cooking the sauce over medium heat until it has reduced by half, about 2 more minutes.

Pour the sauce over the mussels. Garnish with Salsa Fresca, if you wish.

NOTE

Since the shellfish needs room to open, only two servings can be made in one pan. For additional servings, just repeat the process. If you're feeling adventurous, double the recipe and cook it in two separate pans simultaneously!

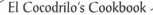

Tostones

Serves 4

These firm, golden-fried plantain patties are easy to make and very versatile. They make great appetizers, or you can serve them as accompaniments to an entrée: place them along side Seafood Ceviche (page 108) for a knock-out combination or with Black Beans Otomí (page 104) and Crème Fraîche (page 40). Tostones are the perfect utensils for any of the fresh salsas—they make great scoops.

> **2 medium-size green plantains,**
>   **sliced in 1-inch thick segments**
>   **(about 6 slices per plantain)**
> **Peanut oil for frying**
> **Salt, to taste**

Heat 2 inches of oil in a deep fryer or deep, heavy skillet to 350°F. Carefully add the plantain sections to the hot oil. Fry until they are golden brown and begin to float, about 5 minutes.

Remove the plantains from the oil; drain on paper towels. Salt to taste while hot. Place each plantain section between two pieces of waxed paper or two cloth napkins; press the plantain with the heel of your hand, forming a little golden patty about ¼-inch thick.

Place each fried plantain between two pieces of waxed paper. Press plantain with the heel of your hand to form a little golden patty about ¼ inch thick.

NOTE

For extra-crispy tostones, refry the pressed patties, turning once, for 3 minutes.

Casuelitas

Serves 8 to 10

These golden-fried "little pans" (or casseroles) are the perfect containers for any savory filling. This recipe calls for zucchini, but be creative! Try crabmeat, sautéed shrimp, Avocado Salsa (page 64), chili, Black Beans Otomí (page 104) and Crème Fraîche (page 40).

- **6 tablespoons Chipotle Chile Butter (page 55)**
- **2 pounds zucchini, diced**
- **4 tablespoons freshly grated Parmesan cheese**
- **2 cups mashed potatoes**
- **2 cups cooked masa harina***
- **Peanut or vegetable oil for frying**

Melt the butter in a 12-inch skillet. Add the zucchini; cook, over medium heat, stirring often, until soft, 3 to 4 minutes. Add the cheese; stir and remove from the heat immediately. Set aside.

Mix the mashed potatoes and masa harina in a large bowl. Shape the mixture into 20 balls, about 1½ ounces each. Press your thumb deeply into the center of each ball; continue shaping the dough, pinching and rotating it, to form a little "pan" that is 2½ inches in diameter and ½ inch deep.

Press your thumb deeply into the center of each ball; continue pinching and rotating the dough until you form a little "pan" 2½ inches in diameter, with ½-inch sides.

Heat 2 inches of oil in a deep fryer or deep, heavy skillet, to 375°F. Fry 6 to 7 casuelitas at a time (do not overcrowd the pan) until golden brown, 4 minutes. Drain on paper towels. Repeat until all the casuelitas are fried.

Fill the casuelitas evenly with the zucchini mixture. Serve immediately.

---

*To prepare masa harina, mix with warm water in a 4:3 ratio (for example, 1 cup masa to ¾ cup warm water). The mixture should be the consistency of pie dough. Add more water if needed. For more on masa harina, see page 150.

Guacamole

Makes 3 cups

Serve in a bowl garnished with 2 or 3 thin slices of lime or a sprig of cilantro. It tastes great with tortilla chips, Flautas (page 79), or Tostones (page 81). It also makes a great garnish for tacos, tostadas, fajitas, enchiladas, and other Mexican entrées.

- 2 large ripe Haas avocados, mashed
- 1/4 cup freshly squeezed lemon juice
- 1/3 cup diced onions
- 2 teaspoons minced serrano or jalapeño chiles
- 1/3 cup diced red bell pepper
- 1/2 cup diced tomato
- 1 teaspoon salt
- 1/2 teaspoon freshly ground black pepper
- 1 tablespoon chopped fresh cilantro

Combine the avocado and lemon juice in a medium-size bowl; mix well. Add the remaining ingredients to the avocado mixture; stir until uniformly mixed. Refrigerate, covered, in an airtight container until ready to use.

How to Keep Guacamole from Turning Brown

- Reserve the avocado pit and place it in the bowl with the guacamole.
- Sprinkle lemon juice over the exposed surface of the guacamole; mix well before serving.
- Keep the guacamole tightly covered and refrigerated.

Spicy Roasted Peanuts

Makes 2 cups

Whip up Spicy Roasted Peanuts to use as a garnish and to add crunch and zing to casseroles. Serve them as a finger food with soft drinks, beers, or cocktails. It is important to use habanero hot sauce or another thick hot pepper sauce in this recipe; Tabasco sauce will make the nuts soggy.

- One 1-pound canned honey roasted peanuts
- 2 tablespoons habanero hot sauce

Preheat the oven to 300°F.

Combine the peanuts and habanero sauce in a small bowl; toss until the peanuts are well coated. Spread onto a cookie sheet; bake until the peanuts are dry and crunchy, 6 to 10 minutes.

Cool uncovered. Store cooled nuts, covered, in an airtight container.

Tostaditas

If you don't have Chicken Criollo on hand, any leftover shredded beef, pork, lamb, shrimp, or seafood will do as tasty substitutions. Or try crumbled, cooked chorizo or linguiza sausage.

> 2 cups mashed potatoes
> 2 cups cooked masa harina (page 150)
> Peanut oil for frying
> ¾ cup Green Cashew Sauce (page 58)
> 2 cups shredded Chicken Breast Criollo
>   with Mango Salsa (page 121)
> 1¼ cups Salsa Brava (page 52)

Mix the mashed potatoes and masa harina in a large bowl. Shape the mixture into 30 balls, about 1 ounce each. Flatten each ball with the fingers of your hand to form a circle about 2½ inches in diameter; press the edges up to form a small lip around the edge of the circle.

Flatten each ball with your fingertips to form a circle about 2½ inches in diameter.

Heat 2 inches of oil in a deep fryer or deep, heavy skillet, to 370°F. Fry 6 to 7 tostaditas at a time (do not overcrowd the pan) until golden brown on the outside, 3 to 5 minutes. Drain on paper towels. Repeat until all the tostaditas are fried.

Spread about 1 teaspoon of the Green Cashew Sauce on each tostadita; top with 1 tablespoon of the Chicken Criollo. Garnish with 2 teaspoons of Salsa Brava. Serve warm.

Spicy Pecans

Use these nuts as beer or cocktail accompaniments or as a garnish on green salads or pastas. Before storing the nuts, be sure they have cooled completely, or they'll loose their crunchiness.

> 2 tablespoons butter
> 1 teaspoon olive oil
> 1 pound whole pecans
> 1 tablespoon crushed red pepper flakes

Combine the butter and oil in a 10-inch skillet; cook, over medium heat, until the butter melts. Add the pecans to the butter mixture; cook, stirring frequently, 10 minutes. Add the red pepper flakes; cook, stirring frequently, 5 more minutes. Remove from the heat; drain the excess oil. Cool. Store the nuts, covered, in an airtight container.

Chicha de Piña

Serves 4

This tropical American beverage is a great nonalcoholic accompaniment to barbecue, seafood, and spicy Mexican entrées as well as an excellent choice for luncheons. It can be served either hot or cold. Since it uses the skin and the core of a fresh pineapple (which are usually discarded) it's the perfect way to get the maximum yield from the "king of fruits." So the next time you buy a fresh, whole pineapple to make a salsa or a dessert, save the core and skin and enjoy this drink!

1 fresh, ripe pineapple, fruit removed (reserve for another use), skin and core chopped

2 tablespoons coarsely chopped ginger root

6 cups water

¾ cup sugar

2 tablespoons freshly squeezed lime juice

Mint sprigs, optional

Cinnamon sticks, optional

Combine the pineapple skin and core, ginger, and water in a medium saucepan; bring to a boil. Add ½ cup of the sugar, reduce the heat to low, and simmer until the flavors are released, about 15 minutes. Remove from the heat.

Place the pineapple mixture in a food processor or blender; coarsely chop. Place a medium-size sieve over a medium-size bowl, add the chopped pineapple mixture, and strain. Reserve the liquid; discard the solids. Cool.

When the liquid has cooled, add the lime juice. Sweeten to taste with the remaining sugar; the drink should be slightly tart. Serve chilled, garnished with mint sprigs, if desired. Or heat gently before serving, and garnish with cinnamon sticks, if desired.

Cooking with the King of Fruits

Pineapples contain bromelain, an enzyme that breaks down protein. This means that meats marinated in fresh pineapple will be tender, but gelatin dishes will not set. Don't mix fresh pineapple with dairy products until the last minute.

CROCODILES

Crocodiles belong to a group of reptiles called crocodilians, which includes alligators and gharials. These animals date back to the Upper Triassic period, some two hundred million years ago. Crocodiles saw the arrival of the dinosaurs—they most likely dined on them—and witnessed the extinction of those great lizards. Today, crocodiles are the world's largest reptiles. While most reptiles have very small brains, crocodilians have relatively large brains and are thought to be the most intelligent reptiles of all. These animals exhibit many subtle and complex behaviors on a par with those of birds and mammals. Because crocodilians continue to grow throughout their lives—and some may live beyond one hundred years in the wild—males can reach more than fifteen feet in length and weigh greater than five hundred pounds. (A saltwater crocodile captured off the coast of India was reported to have measured more than twenty-seven feet long and weighed over one thousand pounds.) All crocodilians have at least sixty strong sharp teeth, which they use to capture their prey. They are able to replace lost or worn out teeth by growing new ones. A single croc may go through as many as three thousand teeth in its lifetime.

The American crocodile, *Crocodylus acutus,* can be found in the waters of northern Peru and Venezuela, north along the coasts of Central America and Mexico to Jamaica, Hispanola, Cuba, and the southern tip of Florida. American crocodiles are not known to be aggressive; in fact they prefer to stay as far away from people as possible. Attacks by American crocodiles on humans are almost unheard of.

Crocodiles are excellent hunters: They're fast, strong, and very good at stalking their prey without being seen. Because their eyes and nostrils are on top of their heads, they can remain almost totally submerged while they swim up to their prey, surprising their dinner before it has a chance to realize what has happened. Crocodiles usually eat turtles, small mammals, and birds.

Nesting time for the crocodiles begins in late January and continues through March. The females choose their sites carefully, sometimes searching for weeks along sandy beaches before finding the right spot. Having chosen a nesting site, the female digs a hole in the sand (twelve to sixteen inches deep) in which to lay her eggs. Then, in the middle of the night, she lays a clutch of about twenty-three eggs, covers them, and leaves them to incubate in the warm sand for eighty-five to ninety days.

The temperature of the nest will determine the sex of the crocodiles. Nest temperatures above 91° or below 88°F will produce males, while mid-range nest temperatures around 89°F will produce females. Therefore, in many nests, unless the temperature differs between the layers of eggs, crocodile siblings will be all the same sex.

Toward the end of the incubation period, the female crocodile makes nightly visits to the nest. When she hears the grunts of her hatching offspring, she digs open the nest. She may gently crack the eggs with her jaws to help free the emerging young, then the female picks up the hatchlings in her mouth and carries them to the water. Crocodile specialist Dr. John Thorbjarnarson notes that in protected lagoons, the young crocs may stay together in pods near their mothers for as long as a year. The presence of the adult female croc keeps hungry predators such as hawks and herons away from the little ones.

One species of New World crocodile, the Orinoco crocodile, is on the 1993 Top Ten Most Endangered Species list issued by the World Wildlife Fund. This crocodile, like many others, has been hunted for its hide, has had its habitat invaded, and has been shot as vermin so that today its numbers are severely reduced. To reestablish this species, the Wildlife Conservation Society (founded in 1895 as the New York Zoological Society) has funded the Orinoco Crocodile Project to breed and rear these crocs in captivity and then release them back into the wild. Santos Lusardo National Park and its research station have been established in Venezuela to protect the Orinoco crocodile population. At last report, two thousand captive-bred crocs have been released into the Capanaparo River.

Bradypus tridactylus

SOUPS, CHOWDERS, AND GUMBOS

Bahamian Seafood Chowder

Serves 10 to 12

This is El Cocodrilo's tangy version of the traditional Boston clam chowder; it includes more seafood and a spicy kick. If you are using canned clams, drain them first, reserving the liquid, and check that you have 1 pound of clam meat. Add the reserved liquid to the broth. Feel free to substitute little-necks, count necks, or small cockles for the Manila clams. You can also substitute half-and-half, milk, or evaporated nonfat milk for the heavy cream to save on calories and fat.

- 3 pounds Manila clams, washed and purged*
- 3 quarts water
- 1 pound chopped clams, fresh, frozen, or canned (reserve the liquid, if using canned)
- 1/4 cup peanut or vegetable oil
- 4 stalks celery, chopped
- 1 1/4 medium onions, chopped
- 1/4 teaspoon dried thyme
- 2 crushed bay leaves
- 1 cup Roux (page 39)
- 4 medium potatoes, peeled and diced into 1-inch cubes
- 3/4 cup (6 ounces) scallops
- 3/4 cup (6 ounces) rock shrimp
- Pinch of salt and freshly ground pepper to taste
- 2 quarts heavy cream
- 1 cup Salsa Fresca (page 53)

Combine the Manila clams and water in a large stock pot; cook over high heat, bringing the liquid to a boil. Remove from the heat.

Place a large sieve over a large pot. Strain the clam mixture, reserving both the liquid and the clams (be careful not to add any sand that may have settled to bottom of the pot).

Remove the clams from the shells; set the meat aside and discard the shells. In a small bowl, combine the Manila clams and chopped clams. Set aside.

Heat the oil in a large pot. Add the celery, onions, thyme, and bay leaves; cook over medium heat until the onions are soft, about 5 minutes. Add the clams to the onion mixture; cook, stirring frequently, 2 minutes.

Add the strained broth and reserved liquid, if you used canned clams, to the clam mixture; simmer until the clams are tender, about 15 minutes.

Remove 1 cup of clam broth from the pot; allow it to cool to warm. Combine the Roux with the warm clam broth in a small bowl; whisk until the Roux has dissolved. Pour the Roux mixture into the pot with the clams; gently stir until well combined.

Add the potatoes; simmer for 10 minutes. Add the scallops and rock shrimp; continue simmering until the potatoes are cooked, about 15 minutes. Adjust the seasoning with salt and pepper to taste.

Add the cream; stir to combine thoroughly. Gently heat until warm; serve immediately. Garnish each bowl with about 2 tablespoons of Salsa Fresca.

> Bahamian Seafood Chowder can be made ahead. Don't add the cream, and store the soup in the refrigerator. When you are ready to reheat it, add 2 cups of cream for each quart of the chowder base that you are planning to serve.

---

*To purge clams, place the live clams in cold water for 7 minutes. Change the water and repeat the process two more times. This allows the clams to clean the sand from their systems so it won't end up in your soup.

Bayou Gumbo

Serves 8 to 10

This is everyone's favorite gumbo at El Cocodrilo. It calls for Cajun (andouille) sausage, which is a spicy, heavily smoked sausage traditionally used in gumbo and jambalaya. Enjoy this rich, full-flavored gumbo as a main dish; invite friends over for a casual dinner and serve a make-ahead meal that will win rave reviews.

4 tablespoons peanut oil

2 cups chopped onions

$\frac{1}{2}$ teaspoon crushed red pepper flakes

1 tablespoon salt

$\frac{1}{2}$ teaspoon freshly ground black pepper

$\frac{1}{2}$ teaspoon dried oregano

Pinch of dried thyme

$2\frac{1}{2}$ tablespoons filé powder*

$\frac{1}{2}$ cup brown Roux (page 39)

1 cup Rich Chicken Stock (page 38) dissolved in 3 quarts water

1 can (16 ounces) chili sauce

1 stalk celery, chopped

1 green bell pepper, chopped

1 red bell pepper, chopped

$\frac{1}{2}$ tablespoon minced garlic

2 carrots, diced

2 pounds chicken wings

1 pound Cajun or Polish sausage, cut into $\frac{1}{4}$-inch pieces

1 teaspoon hot red pepper sauce

$\frac{1}{2}$ pound crabmeat

Heat the oil in a large stock pot. Add the onions; cook over medium heat, stirring frequently, until softened, 3 to 5 minutes. Add the red pepper flakes, salt, black pepper, oregano, thyme, filé powder, and Roux; continue to stir. Slowly add the chicken stock, stirring constantly. Add the chili sauce and bring the mixture to a boil. Reduce the heat; simmer 10 minutes to allow the flour to cook.

Add the celery, bell peppers, garlic, carrots, chicken wings, sausage, and red pepper sauce to the broth mixture. Continue to simmer the broth, skimming the fat from the surface every 5 minutes, until the chicken is cooked, about 20 minutes. Just before serving, stir in the crabmeat, and adjust the seasoning. Serve immediately.

Cajun cooking, a combination of French and Southern cuisine, was developed in the bayou country of Louisiana by Cajuns, descendants of Acadians who were forced from their Canadian homeland by the British in 1785. Cajun food is a robust, country-style cooking that uses spices, roux, filé powder, chopped green peppers, onions, and celery as well as pork, crayfish, and seafood.

---

*This powder can be found in the spice section of most supermarkets, or through mail order.

Gulf Port Seafood Gumbo

Serves 8 to 10

Filé, which gives gumbo its distinctive flavor, is readily available in the seasonings section of most supermarkets. To add more kick to this tasty gumbo, increase the amount of serrano chile. If you're substituting larger shrimp or oysters, be sure to cut them in half. Rich, thick, and hearty, this gumbo makes a great main dish; just add a green salad and some crusty French bread—and dinner is served!

4 rounded tablespoons filé powder
$\frac{1}{2}$ teaspoon crushed red pepper flakes
$\frac{1}{2}$ teaspoon dried oregano
1 teaspoon freshly ground black pepper
Pinch of dried thyme
2 tablespoons vegetable oil
$1\frac{1}{2}$ cups chopped onions
1 serrano or jalapeño chile, diced
$2\frac{1}{2}$ teaspoons minced garlic
$\frac{3}{4}$ cup Roux (page 39) at room temperature
10 cups clam juice or shellfish broth
$\frac{1}{2}$ cup ($\frac{1}{4}$ pound) bay scallops
10 ounces diced fresh Pacific snapper (rock cod)
1 cup ($\frac{1}{2}$ pound) bay shrimp or rock shrimp
1 cup ($\frac{1}{2}$ pound) shelled small fresh Pacific oysters
$\frac{1}{2}$ red bell pepper, diced
$\frac{1}{2}$ green bell pepper, diced

Combine the filé powder, red pepper flakes, oregano, black pepper, and thyme in a small bowl. Mix well; set aside.

Heat the oil in a 10-inch skillet. Add the onions; cook over medium heat, until soft, about 3 to 5 minutes. Add the chile, garlic, and reserved spice mixture to the onions; continue to cook, stirring often. Add the Roux; mix to coat the onion mixture.

Slowly add the clam juice, stirring constantly with a wire whisk, until the Roux and spices are evenly blended in the liquid. Allow the liquid to come to a slow boil; reduce the heat to low; simmer until the liquid thickens, about 15 minutes. Add the scallops, snapper, shrimp, and oysters; cook 1 to 2 minutes. Add the bell peppers; cook for another 5 minutes. Serve immediately.

Ham and Oyster Gumbo

Substitute $\frac{3}{4}$ cup Rich Chicken Stock (page 38) dissolved in $2\frac{1}{2}$ quarts of water for the clam juice; substitute $3\frac{1}{2}$ cups (1 pound) honey-cured ham, diced, for the scallops, snapper, and shrimp; increase the oysters to 2 cups.

Caldo de Camarones

Shrimp Caldo

Serves 4

This delicious, low-calorie, heart-smart caldo won first place for entrées in the 1993 Art for the Heart cooking competition sponsored by the Carmel Mission Trails Chapter of the American Heart Association.

5 cups water

1 pound large shrimp (page 79), peeled, deveined, and quartered

¼ cup julienned carrots

¼ cup diced celery

2 tablespoons diced red onion

2 teaspoons finely sliced garlic

¼ teaspoon freshly ground black pepper

½ teaspoon crushed red pepper flakes

1 teaspoon salt

½ sprig of fresh mint, with stem (about 5 to 6 large leaves)

⅓ cup fresh or frozen thawed corn kernels

½ cup diced tomato

4 heaping tablespoons Sun-Dried Cranberry Salsa (page 54)

Combine the water, shrimp, carrots, celery, onion, garlic, black pepper, red pepper flakes, salt, and mint in a large saucepan; cook over medium heat, stirring occasionally, until the liquid begins to simmer, 7 to 10 minutes.

Remove the mint sprig; set it aside. Add the corn and tomato to the shrimp mixture; continue to simmer for 2 minutes more.

Chop the reserved mint leaves, and return them to the shrimp mixture; stir well. Serve immediately, garnishing each bowl with 1 heaping tablespoon of Sun-Dried Cranberry Salsa.

Seafood Caldo

Serves 4

1 cup bay scallops, rinsed (about
 ½ pound)

1 cup rock shrimp, rinsed (about
 ½ pound)

Two 8-ounce snapper (rock cod) fillets,
 rinsed and cut into 1-inch cubes

8 mussels in their shells, scrubbed and
 debearded

4 cups water

1 cup diced tomatoes

¼ cup diced red onion

¼ cup diced jícama

¼ cup julienned carrots

1 serrano or jalapeño chile, finely
 minced

2 tablespoons chopped fresh cilantro

4 teaspoons freshly squeezed lime juice

Salt and freshly ground black pepper
 to taste

Combine the cleaned seafood and cold water in a medium saucepan. Cook, over medium heat, until the liquid simmers and mussels open, about 5 minutes (discard any mussels that do not open). Add the tomatoes, onion, jícama, carrots, and chile to the seafood. Bring the liquid to a boil, reduce the heat, and simmer 2 minutes. The vegetables will still be fresh and crisp. Gently stir in the cilantro and lime juice; season with salt and pepper. Serve immediately.

Serrano chiles are small tapered chiles with a snappy fresh bite. If necessary, fresh jalapeño chiles can be substituted one for one.

Zucchini Bisque Barbero

Serves 8 to 10

This dish has the texture and richness of a cream-based soup—but without the calories. This soup freezes very well, so it's a great recipe to use when your garden produces an abundance of zucchini. You can add pasta shells to give the dish a little more body. Top the bisque with Salsa Fresca (page 53) for some added zing.

8 tablespoons Rich Chicken Stock
 (page 38) dissolved in 6 cups water

¾ pound lean bacon, cooked and
 broken into ½-inch pieces

2 dashes Worcestershire sauce

3 pounds (about 15 small) zucchini, cut
 in quarters

4 large carrots, cut in quarters

4 stalks celery, strings removed, cut in
 quarters

5 whole garlic cloves

1 onion, cut in half

2 teaspoons salt

1 teaspoon freshly ground black pepper

2 cups peeled and diced tomatoes

Combine chicken stock, bacon pieces, Worcestershire sauce, zucchini, carrots, celery, garlic, onion, salt, and pepper in a large pot or Dutch oven; bring the liquid to a boil. Reduce the heat to low; simmer, uncovered, 1 hour.

Place the vegetable mixture in a food processor or blender (or use a submersion blender); purée. Return the mixture to the pot; add the tomatoes. Increase the heat to medium-low; slowly bring the liquid to a simmer. Cook 10 minutes; serve immediately.

Sopa de Calabacitas

Spicy Pumpkin Soup

Serves 4

This is a great autumn soup that will really take the chill off of a frosty night. When you buy your pumpkins for Halloween, or if you are lucky enough to have your own pumpkin patch, pick out a few for this delicious soup. To cut calories, substitute evaporated nonfat milk for the heavy cream. This soup is delicious garnished with *Roasted Red Pepper Sauce (page 59)* or *Salsa Fresca (page 53)*; try it topped with *Mango Salsa (page 53)* and chopped fresh pineapple.

> ## Cooking Fresh Pumpkin
>
> Preheat the oven to 350°F. Select a 4- to 5-pound pumpkin, cut it in half, and remove the seeds. Place the pumpkin halves in a large baking dish, cut side up, with about 1 inch of water in the bottom of the dish. Bake until the flesh is tender and can be easily pricked with a fork, about 1½ hours. Remove from the oven and allow to cool. Scoop the pumpkin flesh from the skin, using a large spoon. Use immediately or cover and refrigerate up to 1 week.

- 2 pounds fresh cooked or canned pumpkin (about 4 cups)
- 1 habanero chile (page 150), roasted* and minced
- 3 garlic cloves, minced
- ¼ teaspoon ground cinnamon
- ¼ teaspoon dried thyme
- ¼ teaspoon freshly ground nutmeg or allspice
- ½ cup freshly squeezed orange juice
- 2 tablespoons peanut oil
- 1 red bell pepper, seeded and chopped
- 1 green bell pepper, seeded and chopped
- 1 red onion, diced
- ½ cup Rich Chicken Stock (page 38) dissolved in 4 cups water
- 1 cup heavy cream
- 1 cup fresh or frozen corn kernels
- 2½ teaspoons salt
- Freshly ground black pepper to taste

Combine the pumpkin, chile, garlic, cinnamon, thyme, nutmeg, orange juice, peanut oil, bell peppers, onion, and chicken stock in large saucepan; cook over high heat, bringing the liquid to a boil. Reduce the heat to low; simmer 20 minutes. Remove from the heat.

Pour the broth into a food processor or blender; purée until smooth. Return the puréed broth to the pot. Add the cream and corn; heat gently until warm. Season with salt and pepper.

---

*See "Roasting Peppers" on page 51.

Black Bean Soup

Serves 4

If you are making a pot of Black Beans Otomí, then this soup will be a snap to make. It's a hearty luncheon entrée or a satisfying first course at dinner. Try serving it Mexican-style, topped with a poached egg and freshly grated cheese. Salsa Fresca (page 53), Crème Fraîche (page 40), and sour cream also make wonderful garnishes.

    1 tablespoon olive oil

    ½ onion, chopped

    ½ serrano or jalapeño chile, diced

    1 teaspoon minced garlic

    5 cups liquid strained from Black Beans Otomí (page 104)

    ½ cup cooked black beans

Heat the oil in a large pot. Add the onion, chile, and garlic; cook over medium heat, stirring frequently, until the onions are soft, 3 to 5 minutes. Add the liquid and black beans to the onion mixture; continue cooking until the flavors are well blended, 15 to 20 minutes. Serve immediately.

Two Recipes in One!

This recipe is an accompaniment to the recipe for Black Beans Otomí (page 104). Just at the point when the black beans are almost cooked (they are usually pretty thick at this point, since most of the liquid in the pot has been reduced and absorbed), add 6 cups of water, stir well, and allow the mixture to come to a full simmer. (If your beans are cooked and you still have a lot of unabsorbed liquid in the pot, don't add any more.) The liquid should be a rich brown. Strain off 5 cups of the liquid.

SLOTHS

The sloth is a shaggy mammal whose face looks something like the Wookie in the *Star Wars* films. This dog-size animal has developed some very unique adaptations to life in the rain forest canopy. The sloth has strong, hooked claws, which are used to grip the branches of trees. With these powerful claws locked around a branch, the sloth can hang upside down, motionless, for hours at a stretch. This grip is so strong that even after a sloth dies, the animal will remain suspended from the tree branch high above the forest floor. For this reason, forest peoples usually won't waste their time hunting sloths, knowing that even if they shoot the animal, they won't be able to get it down, even by shaking the tree. In the constant humidity and regular downpour of the rain forest, the sloth remains relatively dry because its fur grows from its belly toward its backbone (the reverse of other mammals). So when it rains, the water just runs off the shaggy fur of the upside-down animal.

Sloths are famous for their lethargy; they even sneeze in slow motion. In fact, they are the slowest-moving mammals on earth. A female sloth was recorded moving at a speed of 5 yards a minute, less than $\frac{1}{5}$ mile per hour, while hurrying to her distressed baby!

Sloths spend their whole lives in the trees. There they eat, sleep (about eighteen 18 hours a day), and just hang there motionless. Unlike most mammals, a sloth's body temperature varies with the environment so sloths hang in sunny openings in the forest canopy to absorb the heat of the sun.

Sloths seem to be designed for immobility. The three-toed sloth has nine vertebrae in its neck, two more than most mammals, which enables it to turn its head in almost every direction (about 270°). So, hanging from a branch, the sloth can twist its head to browse on its favorite cecropia tree without even moving its body.

Sloths even mate and give birth to their young while suspended from branches. The newborn sloth has tiny claws, which it uses to grip onto its mother's belly soon after birth. Cradled in its mother's arms, wrapped in her limbs and shaggy hair, the newborn sloth is warm and well protected—and scarcely visible. For a month or two the baby sloth will hitch a ride with its mother, but soon it learns to move slowly about by itself; by five months, the little sloth has mastered the art of hanging around on its own.

Gentle and peaceful, sloths are relatively defenseless. Their best protection against their enemies is actually their very slowness and their protective coloration. They are hard to detect, since they move so slowly; they even have algae growing in their fur, which further camouflages them against the backdrop of the forest. The algae grows in the grooves of the sloth's hairs, giving the animals a green tint in wet conditions. In times of drought, the algae turns yellow, allowing the sloths to blend in with the scenery around them as the seasons change. With its head down on its chest, a sleeping sloth looks a lot like a bunch of dried leaves. If they are attacked, sloths can defend themselves by biting and by slashing with their hooked claws, but they usually protect themselves against their enemies—jaguars, ocelots, tree snakes, and birds of prey—by curling up into impenetrable balls.

Besides the green algae growing on their hair, sloths also support and provide camouflage for the various species of moths, ticks, beetles, fleas, and mites who live in their fur. Several hundred insects may live on one individual sloth. One particular species of moth is found only in the sloth's fur and is thought to feed on the algae growing there.

Sloths rarely come down to the forest floor; on the ground they are almost helpless against their enemies since they cannot run or even walk. They must pull themselves along by their hooked claws, dragging their bellies on the ground. The muscles in their legs, adapted to hanging from tree limbs, are too weak for walking, and their curved claws inhibit standing upright. In spite of the difficulty sloths have maneuvering on land, they make a trip to the forest floor once a week. Three-toed sloths digest their meals slowly and defecate only once a week; they bury their droppings, as cats do. They climb down to the base of a tree and dig a hole in the ground with augerlike motions of their short, blunt tails. By burying their waste, the sloths are actually performing a service to the rain forest; they are recycling what they have consumed and planting the seeds of the fruits they have eaten so that a new generation of trees can take root.

NOTE

One unusual aspect of sloths that may prove particularly beneficial to humans is their vital resistance to infection. Serious wounds heal quickly and rarely become infected. Scientists are studying sloths to learn how this biological mechanism works.

PANTHERA ONCA

SIDES AND SALADS

Costa Rican Rice

Serves 6 to 8

The rice should be fluffy and mildly tasty when done. It's a perfect side dish for many of the entrées in this book.

- 1 tablespoon peanut oil
- $1/3$ cup diced red or green bell pepper
- $1/2$ cup diced onion
- 2 cups long grain rice, well rinsed
- $1\,1/3$ cups water
- 2 teaspoons tomato paste
- $1/4$ teaspoon freshly ground black pepper
- 2 teaspoons salt
- 2 tablespoons freshly squeezed lime juice
- 1 teaspoon olive oil

Heat the peanut oil in a medium saucepan. Add the bell pepper and onion; cook over medium heat, stirring often, until the onion begins to brown. Add the rice, water, tomato paste, black pepper, salt, and lime juice; mix well. Bring the liquid to a boil. Add the olive oil to the rice mixture; reduce the heat, and simmer, covered and undisturbed, until all the liquid is absorbed, about 20 minutes. Serve hot.

Coconut Lime Rice

Serves 4

This is the perfect complement to any seafood dish or chicken entrée—and it's delicious on its own too!

- 3 cups water
- 2 cups shredded sweetened coconut
- 1 tablespoon olive oil
- 1 cup Basmati rice
- 1 teaspoon salt
- $1/4$ teaspoon freshly ground black pepper
- 2 tablespoons freshly squeezed lime juice

Combine the water and shredded coconut in a small saucepan; simmer over medium heat for 5 minutes. Place a small strainer over a small bowl. Strain the coconut mixture; reserve the liquid; discard the solids. Set aside.

Heat the oil in a 8-inch skillet; add the rice. Cook over medium heat until the grains of rice begin to change from clear to solid white on the ends, about 7 minutes.

Add 2 cups of the reserved coconut liquid to the rice; bring to a boil. Add the salt, pepper, and lime juice. Reduce the heat; simmer, covered and undisturbed, until all the liquid is absorbed, about 20 minutes.

Black Beans Otomí

Serves 6

Crème Fraîche (page 40) and Salsa Fresca (page 53) make a super garnish for this dish.

1 pound dry black beans, sorted, rinsed, and drained

1 cup chopped onions

¼ cup peanut oil

2 tablespoons minced garlic

2 serrano or jalapeño chiles, halved

½ cup Rich Chicken Stock (page 38) dissolved in 2 quarts water

1 teaspoon salt or to taste

Freshly ground black pepper to taste

Combine the beans, onions, oil, garlic, chiles, and Rich Chicken Stock in a large, heavy stock pot or clay pot; bring the liquid to a slow boil. Reduce the heat to low, and simmer, stirring occasionally, until the beans soften and the stock thickens, about 4 hours. Season with salt and pepper; cook 1 hour, adding more liquid if necessary. Remove the chiles before serving.

Vegetarian Black Beans

Place 4 to 5 bay leaves, 4 carrots, 1 cup chopped onions, 1 cup chopped red or green bell peppers, and 2 quarts water in a large stock pot. Simmer over low heat for 30 minutes until the vegetables are tender. Remove and discard the bay leaves; purée the mixture in a food processor or blender until smooth. Substitute the puréed mixture for the Rich Chicken Stock.

Tips for Great Beans

- Carefully sort through the dry beans. Often, small rocks are inadvertently included in the package and are hard to distinguish from the beans (until you bite into one!).

- Use a clay pot, if you have one, and your beans will be even more flavorful. Generations of Latin cooks swear by this!

- Don't add salt to the beans until the last hour of simmering time. Salt will toughen the skins if added too early, and it will also increase cooking time.

- Season carefully! Beans need salt or they will taste very flat. As a rule of thumb, start with 1 teaspoon salt for 1 pound of beans and go from there. Just remember to add the salt in the last hour of cooking .

- While cooking beans, slow and easy is best. Let them simmer on a very low heat, uncovered. There's nothing worse than a pot of scorched beans. Stir occasionally and add 1 to 2 cups of water when necessary.

Scallop and Shrimp Pasta Salad

VVVVVVVVVVVVVVVVVV

Serves 8 to 10

Serve this salad on a bed of lettuce leaves and garnish it with parsley and/or freshly grated Parmesan cheese. This salad makes an excellent luncheon or buffet dish. If you wish to cut calories, use a low-calorie mayonnaise or subsitute 1 cup of your favorite low-calorie dressing for the vinaigrette.

1½ pounds fresh tricolor fusilli (cork-screw pasta)

1 cup mayonnaise

⅓ cup red wine vinegar

6 tablespoons prepared pesto

½ teaspoon dried oregano

½ teaspoon salt

1 teaspoon freshly ground black pepper

1 roasted red bell pepper,* diced

1 roasted green bell pepper,* diced

½ red onion, diced

1 cup grated carrots

¼ pound cooked bay shrimp**

¼ pound cooked bay scallops†

½ cup freshly grated Parmesan cheese (garnish)

Place the pasta in a large pot of boiling water; cook until al dente, 10 to 12 minutes. Drain; rinse with cool water. Transfer to a large bowl.

Meanwhile, combine the mayonnaise, vinegar, pesto, oregano, salt, and pepper in a small bowl; mix well.

Add the bell peppers, onion, and carrots to the cooked pasta. Add the mayonnaise mixture to the pasta mixture; blend well. Add the shrimp and scallops; stir to blend. Chill the salad well before serving. Garnish with Parmesan cheese.

---

*See "Roasting Peppers" on page 51.

**Precooked bay shrimp can be found in the freezer section of most supermarkets; just make sure you don't cook them twice!

†To cook raw scallops, place the scallops in 1 quart boiling water; reduce the heat, and simmer until just cooked (they will turn white, opaque, and firm). Remove from the heat, drain, and cool in cold water.

Pesto . . . Presto!

Pesto is available in the freezer section of many supermarkets, but it's very easy to make. Pesto is a wonderful way to save the flavor of fresh summer basil for winter meals. To preserve the color of the pesto, stir in 1 tablespoon of freshly squeezed lemon juice during final minute of blending.

½ cup firmly packed fresh basil

3 garlic cloves

¼ cup pine nuts or walnuts

¼ cup grated aged Parmesan cheese (optional)

½ cup olive oil

Salt to taste

Place the basil, garlic, pine nuts, and cheese in a food processor or blender; process until finely chopped. With the motor running, add the oil in a thin, steady stream until the mixture forms a smooth paste and is well blended, 2 to 3 minutes. Refrigerate, covered.

Quinoa Cano

Serves 4

Serve this dish as an accompaniment to seafood or meat entrées; garnish each serving with a tablespoon of one of your favorite salsas.

- 1 tablespoon olive oil
- 1 tablespoon minced garlic
- ½ cup minced onion
- 1 serrano or jalapeño chile, minced
- 2 cups quinoa, well rinsed
- 2 tablespoons Rich Chicken Stock (page 38) dissolved in 2½ cups water
- 2 teaspoons salt

Heat the oil in a medium saucepan. Add the garlic, onion, and chile; cook, over medium heat, until the onion begins to soften, 3 to 5 minutes. Add the quinoa, Rich Chicken Stock, and salt; bring the mixture to a boil. Reduce the heat to low; simmer, covered and undisturbed, until all the liquid has been absorbed, about 20 minutes. Serve hot.

Quinoa, The Super Grain

Quinoa, pronounced KEEN-wa, has the highest protein content of any grain. It is also high in lysine, an amino acid that is scarce in the vegetable kingdom. One serving of this great grain—about one cup—will provide you with 6 grams of protein and 20 percent of your daily iron requirement, and has only 138 calories and just 2 grams of fat. See the note on page 107 regarding washing quinoa.

Wild Rice and Posole Salad

Serves 8 to 10

This recipe is actually a combination of wild rice salsa and posole salsa, and it makes a great salad or a vegetarian entrée. Canned chipotle chiles (smoked jalapeño chiles) are available in Latin groceries or a well-stocked supermarket. Hominy will be found in the canned vegetable section of the supermarket and in Latin groceries. White and yellow hominy are interchangeable, so don't panic if you can only find one variety; just double the amount, and you're good to go.

- 1 cup wild rice
- 4 cups water
- ½ cup canned yellow hominy, rinsed and drained
- ½ cup canned white hominy, rinsed and drained
- 1 cup diced red bell pepper
- 1½ chipotle chiles, minced
- 2½ cups Salsa Fresca (page 53)
- 4 tablespoons chopped fresh cilantro
- 1 cup freshly squeezed lime juice
- 4 tablespoons olive oil
- 2½ tablespoons sugar
- ¼ teaspoon salt

Combine the rice and water in a medium saucepan; cook over medium heat until the rice grains open, about 1 hour. Remove from the heat; drain. Transfer the rice to a large bowl and place it in the refrigerator to cool.

Combine the remaining ingredients and the cooled rice; mix well. Cover and refrigerate for 8 hours, allowing the flavors to marry. Serve chilled.

Quinoa Summer Salad

Serves 12

This is a great dish to carry along to a family reunion, a summer picnic, a church social, or school pot luck. The recipe serves 12, but it can be halved to serve 6. Don't let the long list of ingredients deter you from trying this delicious salad; there is actually very little prep work so the salad can be made quite easily from a well-stocked pantry.

1 teaspoon peanut or vegetable oil

¼ cup diced yellow onion

1 tablespoon minced garlic

Pinch of crushed red pepper flakes

2½ cups water

3 teaspoons salt

½ teaspoon freshly ground black pepper

2 cups quinoa, well rinsed

½ cup diced red bell pepper

¾ cup diced jícama

¾ cup diced tomato

2 teaspoons minced serrano or jalapeño chiles

¾ cup julienned carrots

½ cup fresh or frozen thawed sweet corn kernels

¼ cup diced red onion

4½ teaspoons chopped fresh cilantro

1 tablespoon chopped fresh mint or basil

2 tablespoons olive oil

3 tablespoons balsamic vinegar*

Heat the peanut oil in a medium saucepan. Add the yellow onion and garlic; cook over medium heat until the onion begins to soften, 3 to 5 minutes. Add the red pepper flakes; cook 1 minute more.

Add the water, 2 teaspoons of the salt, and ¼ teaspoon of the black pepper to the onion mixture; bring to a boil. Mix in the quinoa; reduce the heat to low and simmer, covered and undisturbed, 20 minutes. Remove from the heat; drain any remaining water and transfer the mixture to a medium-size bowl. Set aside to cool.

Combine the cooled quinoa, the remaining salt and ¼ teaspoon of pepper, and the remaining ingredients in a large bowl; mix well. Chill before serving.

> **NOTE**
>
> Make sure you rinse quinoa thoroughly before using it. The grain is coated with a natural insecticide, saponin, produced by the plant, which makes it taste bitter to insects (and us). Water easily removes it.

---

*For this recipe, do not substitute another type of vinegar for the balsamic vinegar.

Seafood Ceviche

Serves 4

If you prefer, use any combination of fresh scallops, shrimp, and fish to equal 1 pound instead of using scallops only. It is very important that the seafood be as fresh as possible, since it is "cooked" in the citrus juices. Serve each portion with a quarter slice of avocado and a lime wedge. It's best to eat this dish on the same day that it's made.

- 1 pound fresh scallops
- 1/2 cup freshly squeezed lemon juice
- 1/4 cup freshly squeezed Seville orange juice*
- 1/2 cup diced red onion, rinsed in cold water after dicing
- 1/2 teaspoon minced garlic
- 1/2 cup diced peeled, seeded, and drained tomato
- 2 serrano chiles, finely diced
- 1/2 cup diced red bell pepper
- 1/4 teaspoon freshly ground black pepper
- Salt to taste

Cut the scallops into 1/2-inch cubes. Combine the scallops and lemon juice in a large plastic bag or nonreactive bowl. Cover and refrigerate for 6 hours. Drain the scallops; transfer to a large bowl.

Combine remaining ingredients with the scallops; mix well. Adjust the seasoning with salt and additional black pepper, to taste. Serve immediately.

---

*If you can't find Seville oranges, substitute the freshly squeezed juices of 1/4 grapefruit, 1/2 orange, and 1 lime to make 1/4 cup of juice.

Mixed Greens with Spicy Pecans and Honey-Mustard Vinaigrette

Serves 4

- 6 cups mixed baby greens, rinsed and dried
- 8 cherry tomatoes, halved
- 24 Spicy Pecans (page 86)
- 3/4 cup Honey-Mustard Vinaigrette (below)

Arrange 1 1/2 cups of the mixed greens on each of four plates. Top each salad with 6 Spicy Pecans and 4 tomato halves. Spoon 2 tablespoons of the Honey Mustard Vinaigrette over each salad and serve.

Honey Mustard Vinaigrette

Makes 2 cups

This tasty little vinaigrette will keep for weeks in the refrigerator, just shake well before using.

- 10 tablespoons (5 ounces) red wine vinegar
- 6 tablespoons country-style Dijon mustard
- 1 tablespoon honey
- 1 teaspoon salt
- 1/2 teaspoon freshly ground black pepper
- 1 1/4 cups peanut oil

Combine vinegar, mustard, honey, salt, and pepper in a container with a tight-fitting lid. Cover and shake well. Add the oil and shake until there is no visible separation between the oil and other ingredients. Refrigerate any remaining dressing.

JAGUARS

aguars are the most powerful predatory animals of the Americas. Their heavily muscled bodies are adept at either climbing in trees or swimming in rivers. They will chase prey into the water or swim looking for turtles, fish, and even crocodiles. Jaguars can survive in a variety of terrains—forests, mountains, grasslands, and even swamplands—and they can sustain themselves with a variety of foods, from large herd animals to small insects. While jaguars usually weigh from 100 to 250 pounds, these incredibly strong cats have been seen dragging full-grown horses for more than a mile.

Jaguars are master hunters. Equipped with excellent night vision, sensitive ears that turn in different directions to pick up sound, quiet padded feet for moving silently through the forest, whiskers to act as sensors in the dark, and strong muscles for running quickly, jaguars' bodies are specialized for nocturnal hunting.

NOTE

You can tell jaguars from leopards by their spots. The jaguar has small black spots arranged in rosettes, with usually one or two extra spots in the rosette's center; the leopard's rosettes are usually empty in the center.

While they swim and climb with ease, jaguars usually stalk their prey on the ground, creeping close then pouncing swiftly. They seize their prey with strong forelegs and then kill it with one bite through the head or neck with their sharp canine teeth.

The jaguars are also known as clever hunters. Amazonian forest dwellers believe the jaguar catches fish by deliberately dangling its tail in the water to bait the fish; then, when the fish rise to the surface, the jaguar flings the fish onto the riverbank with its paws.

Jaguars are solitary and secretive; they mark their territory by scratching trees and leaving scent marks. The cats come together at mating time, and after about three months, the female gives birth to two or three kittens. Like all cats, the kittens are born blind and helpless. They stay with their mother for over a year, learning to hunt and fend for themselves. When they mature, they move off of their mother's home range and stake out their own territory.

Known as *El Tigre* in the myths and legends of Central and South America, jaguars have long played an important role in the religions of the New World. To the Aztec, the jaguar was the God of the Night, ruler of the underworld; its spotted coat represented the stars of the night sky. To the Canelos Quiche people, *Amasangua*, the spirit of the forest, appears as the elusive black panther. Jaguar skins were worn as symbols of power and prestige by priests, rulers, and nobles in the Inca, Aztec, and Maya worlds and throughout Central and South America.

The jaguar remains an important symbol in the cultural and spiritual lives of many forest peoples today, but no group has identified with the animal to such an extent as the Matses. The Matses are a tribe of hunter-gatherers inhabiting the lowland jungles of northeastern Peru. This fiercely proud and independent people guard the spirit and customs of their ancestors. Their needs are supplied by the forest, and they resist the intrusion of outsiders. The Matses admire the strength, guile, and hunting prowess of the jaguar. To embody the jaguar's spirit, the Matses tattoo their own faces with markings that resemble those of a jaguar. The Matses men wear long bamboo splints in their upper lips, and the women wear them in their noses—like jaguar whiskers.

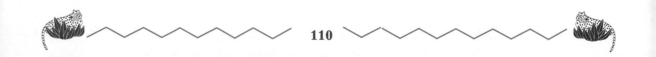

ATELES GEOFFROYI

ENTRÉES

Pecan Crusted Snapper

Serves 4

It is important not to overcrowd the pan while you are cooking these fillets. If your pan cannot accommodate all the fish at one time, just cook it in two batches. It doesn't take long. For an elegant look, shave the Mango Butter before topping the snapper fillets.

- 2 eggs
- 1 tablespoon water
- 1 teaspoon salt
- ½ teaspoon freshly ground black pepper
- 1½ cups pecans, finely chopped into crumbs
- 4 (6-ounce) snapper fillets, skins removed
- 2 teaspoons olive oil
- 4 tablespoons Mango Butter (page 58)

Beat the eggs with the water, salt, and pepper in a shallow bowl. Spread the pecan crumbs on a flat plate or piece of waxed paper. Pat the snapper fillets dry with paper towels. Dip the fillets in the egg mixture, then dredge in the pecan crumbs, coating both sides well.

Heat 1 teaspoon of the oil in a 12-inch skillet. Add the fillets; cook over medium heat, turning once, until the coating begins to crack and juices run, 7 to 8 minutes, depending on the thickness of the fillets. Top each fillet with 1 tablespoon of Mango Butter, and serve.

Peppered Salmon with Cilantro and Roasted Serrano Aioli

Serves 4

This recipe will make approximately 1¾ cups of the aïoli sauce. You will have sauce left over. If you make the sauce ahead of time, and choose to use the yolks, remember that it must be refrigerated because it contains raw eggs.

- 3 egg yolks or 3 tablespoons mayonnaise
- 1 teaspoon salt
- ¼ cup freshly squeezed lime juice
- 1 garlic clove
- 4 serrano or jalapeño chiles, roasted*
- 1 teaspoon balsamic vinegar
- 5 tablespoons chopped fresh cilantro
- 1 cup high quality extra-virgin olive oil
- 4 (6-ounce) salmon fillets
- 1 teaspoon freshly ground black pepper
- 2 tablespoons peanut oil

To prepare the sauce, place the yolks, salt, juice, garlic, chiles, vinegar, and cilantro in a food processor or blender. Blend until smooth, about 1 to 2 minutes. With the motor running, add the olive oil in a thin, steady stream until all the oil is incorporated. Transfer the sauce to an airtight container; refrigerate until ready to use.

To prepare the fish, season both sides of the fish with the black pepper. Heat the peanut oil in a 12-inch skillet. Add the fish; cook over medium heat, turning once until cooked through, 7 to 8 minutes. Garnish with a dollop of the sauce and a sprig of cilantro.

*See "Roasting Peppers" on page 51.

Bayou Brochette

Serves 4

At El Cocodrilo we use alligator meat in this dish along with the chicken and shrimp. Alligator meat is a firm, slightly chewy, white meat. Not surprisingly, it tastes like chicken; but it has a hint of river in its finish. Alligators, once on the brink of extinction here in the United States, are making a big comeback, especially now that they are being commercially raised. We get our gator meat from an alligator farm in Florida. In this recipe, we've substituted fish for the alligator, but if you can get some gator meat, use it! Since this recipe requires a long marinating time, start the night before.

Marinade

½ cup rice vinegar

1 tablespoon light molasses

2 tablespoons freshly squeezed lime juice

3 tablespoons chopped fresh cilantro

½ teaspoon salt

½ teaspoon habanero chile hot sauce (or other hot sauce)

1 tablespoon light corn syrup

Brochette

8 ounces skinless, boneless chicken breast halves, cut into 8 pieces

8 large shrimp (about 6 ounces), cleaned, shelled, and deveined

½ pound swordfish or shark, cut into 8 cubes

1 green bell pepper, seeded and deveined, and cut into 8 pieces

1 red bell pepper, seeded and deveined, and cut into 8 pieces

1 large onion, cut into 16 pieces

4 cherry tomatoes

Glaze

4 tablespoons dark molasses

2 tablespoons Jamaican Jerk Spices, wet or dry (page 62)

5 tablespoons apricot jam

7 tablespoons light corn syrup

2 tablespoons freshly squeezed lime juice

4 tablespoons + 1 teaspoon cider vinegar

2 tablespoons tamarind paste or mango chutney (page 151)

Combine all ingredients for the marinade in a large plastic container with an airtight lid or gallon-size plastic bag. Add the chicken, shrimp, and fish. Cover or seal; refrigerate for 12 to 16 hours.

Meanwhile, place all the ingredients for the glaze in a food processor or blender; purée until smooth. Store the mixture in the refrigerator in an airtight container for 4 hours.

Preheat the grill for a medium fire. On four metal skewers, alternately thread equal amounts of the bell peppers, onion, and marinated meats. Cap each skewer with a cherry tomato.

Grill the brochettes over medium heat, brushing with the glaze and turning several times, until the chicken is firm, the shrimp have curled, and the fish is flaky, about 10 minutes. Serve immediately.

Before You Grill . . .

Before cooking, review "Barbecuing" on page 42. If you are using wooden skewers instead of metal, soak them in water for 30 minutes so they won't burn on the grill.

Calamari Steak with Roasted Red Pepper Sauce

Serves 4

This is a great way to serve calamari. The delicate, somewhat sweet flavor of squid is enhanced by the rich, tangy Roasted Red Pepper Sauce.

2 eggs
1 tablespoon water
1 teaspoon salt
½ teaspoon freshly ground black pepper
½ cup all-purpose flour
4 (4½- to 5-ounce) calamari steaks
2 tablespoons peanut oil
1 cup Roasted Red Pepper Sauce (page 59)
½ cup diced tomatoes
1 teaspoon chopped fresh parsley

Beat the eggs with the water, salt, and pepper in a shallow bowl. Spread the flour on a flat plate or piece of waxed paper. Set aside.

Lightly pound the steaks between two pieces of plastic wrap or waxed paper with a small mallet to tenderize. Dip the steaks into the egg mixture, then dredge in the flour, coating both sides well.

Heat 1 tablespoon oil in a 12-inch skillet. Add the steaks; cook over medium heat, until the first side is golden brown, about 4 minutes. Turn the steaks; cook 2 minutes more. Add the Roasted Red Pepper Sauce, tomatoes, and parsley; cook until heated through, 1 minute.

Transfer the calamari to a serving plate. Spoon the sauce over the steaks, and serve immediately.

Chicken breasts can be substituted for the calamari: Use 8 skinless, boneless chicken breast halves (1¼ pounds), pounded to a ¼-inch thickness and soaked overnight in 2 cups clam juice.

Blackened Swordfish Steaks with Avocado Salsa

⩔⩔⩔⩔⩔⩔⩔⩔⩔⩔⩔⩔⩔⩔

Serves 4

4 (6- to 7-ounce) swordfish steaks

2 tablespoons Cajun Blackening Spices (page 61)

2 tablespoons peanut or vegetable oil

Avocado Salsa (page 64)

Pat the steaks dry with paper towels. Place the Cajun Blackening Spices in a plastic or paper bag; add one steak. Seal and shake until the steak is well coated with the spice mixture. Repeat with the remaining steaks.

Heat the oil in a 12-inch skillet. Add the steaks; cook over medium heat, turning once, until the spices begin to caramelize and blacken, about 7 minutes. Serve each steak topped with 3 table-spoons of Avocado Salsa.

Fettuccine with Shrimp and Green Cashew Sauce

⩔⩔⩔⩔⩔⩔⩔⩔⩔⩔⩔⩔⩔⩔

Serves 4

1½ pounds fresh fettuccine

4 tablespoons olive oil

24 large shrimp (about 1 pound) peeled, cleaned, and deveined

2 teaspoons minced shallots

1 teaspoon minced garlic

½ cup heavy cream

4 tablespoons Green Cashew Sauce (page 58)

1 teaspoon salt

¼ teaspoon freshly ground black pepper

4 rounded tablespoons freshly grated Parmesan cheese

½ cup Salsa Fresca (page 53)

Cook the fettuccine according to the package's directions for *al dente*. Toss the cooked, drained pasta with 2 tablespoons of the oil. Set aside.

Meanwhile, heat the remaining 2 tablespoons of oil in a 12-inch skillet. Add the shrimp; cook over medium heat, until they begin to turn pink, 2 to 3 minutes. Add the shallots and garlic; cook until the shallots soften, 2 to 3 minutes more. Add the cream and Green Cashew Sauce; stir well. Season with salt, pepper, and 2 tablespoons of the cheese.

Add the shrimp mixture to the fettuccine; toss. Serve immediately. Garnish with Salsa Fresca and the remaining cheese.

Amazon Catfish

Serves 4

This dish is like a flavor carnival, combining the fruity Caiman Curry Sauce with the taste of fresh tomatoes and Spicy Roasted Peanuts. Try this with other freshwater fish such as trout and tilapia.

Sauce

1 tablespoon peanut or vegetable oil

1 medium onion, diced

1 cup Caiman Curry Sauce (page 59)

$\frac{1}{2}$ cup diced jícama

$\frac{1}{2}$ cup diced fresh tomatoes, seeded and drained

Fish

2 eggs

1 tablespoon water

1 teaspoon salt

$\frac{1}{2}$ teaspoon freshly ground black pepper

$\frac{1}{2}$ cup all-purpose flour

4 (6-ounce) catfish fillets, with skins removed

1 cup Japanese* or other dried bread crumbs

$\frac{1}{2}$ cup cornmeal

Peanut or vegetable oil for frying

$\frac{1}{4}$ cup Spicy Roasted Peanuts (page 83)

To prepare the sauce, heat the 1 tablespoon oil in a 10-inch skillet. Add the onion; cook over medium heat until golden brown, about 5 minutes. Add the Caiman Curry Sauce; bring the liquid to a boil. Add the jícama and tomatoes to the sauce mixture. Reduce the heat to low; simmer about 2 minutes. Set aside; keep warm.

To prepare the fish, beat the eggs, water, salt, and pepper in a shallow bowl. Spread the flour on a flat plate or piece of waxed paper. Combine the bread crumbs and cornmeal on another flat plate or piece of waxed paper. Dip fillets in the flour and then the egg mixture; then dredge in the bread crumb mixture, coating both sides well.

Heat $\frac{1}{2}$ inch of oil to 350°F in a large, deep, heavy skillet. Carefully add 2 fillets; cook over medium-high heat, turning once, until golden brown, 6 to 8 minutes. Remove with a slotted spoon or spatula; drain on paper towels. Repeat with the remaining fillets. Top the fillets with the warm sauce; garnish with Spicy Roasted Peanuts. Serve immediately.

*Japanese bread crumbs (*panko*) can be found with other bread crumbs and batter mixes in most supermarkets and are available through mail order.

Caribbean-Spiced Mahi Mahi with Habanero-Peach Butter

Serves 4

This dish is a tasty way to prepare saltwater fish; try it with halibut or thresher shark. The Habanero-Peach Butter adds a lightly spicy, fruity accent that complements the flavor of the fish. Grill the fish to make this dish extra-special.

2 medium garlic cloves, minced

½ medium red onion, minced

½ tablespoon ground red pepper

1 tablespoon freshly ground black pepper

1½ tablespoons mild paprika

½ teaspoon dried thyme

½ teaspoon dried oregano

½ teaspoon dried basil

4 (6- to 8-ounce) mahi mahi fillets

4 tablespoons Habanero–Peach Butter (page 56)

Preheat the broiler. Combine the garlic, onion, red pepper, black pepper, paprika, thyme, oregano, and basil in a shallow bowl; mix well.

Dredge the fillets in the spice mixture, coating both sides well. Place the fillets onto a foil-lined baking sheet. Broil 4 inches from the heat, turning once, until the juices begin to run, about 7 minutes. Garnish each fillet with 1 tablespoon of the Habanero-Peach Butter. Serve immediately.

Snapper Mardi Gras

Serves 4

This dish is like a party in your mouth! The Cajun Blackening Spices and the Roasted Red Pepper Sauce dance with the fresh tomatoes and cilantro to make this a memorable seafood dish.

4 (6-ounce) snapper fillets, skin removed

3 tablespoons olive oil

¼ cup Cajun Blackening Spices (page 61)

1 cup Roasted Red Pepper Sauce (page 59)

½ cup diced fresh tomatoes, seeded and drained

2 tablespoons chopped fresh cilantro

Pat the snapper fillets dry with paper towels. Rub the fillets lightly with 1 tablespoon of the oil, just to moisten. Place the Cajun Blackening Spices in a plastic or paper bag; add one fillet. Seal and shake until the fillet is well coated with the spice mixture. Repeat with the remaining fillets.

Heat the remaining 2 tablespoons of oil in a 12-inch skillet. Add the fillets; cook over medium heat, turning once, until they begin to blacken, about 6 minutes. Add the Roasted Red Pepper Sauce and tomatoes; simmer 1 minute. Transfer the fillets to a serving platter; continue cooking the sauce for 2 minutes more. Serve the fillets topped with the sauce and garnished with the cilantro.

Sautéed Prawns Rio Coco

Shrimp in Lime Coconut Sauce

▽▽▽▽▽▽▽▽▽▽▽▽▽▽▽▽▽

Serves 4

1½ cups sweetened shredded coconut

1½ cups water

¼ cup heavy cream

1½ tablespoons olive oil

2 tablespoons finely chopped shallots

1 tablespoon finely chopped garlic

½ serrano or jalapeño chile, finely chopped

36 large shrimp (about 1½ pounds), peeled, deveined, and patted dry

1 cup diced jícama

1 teaspoon chopped fresh parsley

2 tablespoons freshly squeezed lime juice

½ cup sweetened shredded coconut, toasted*

Combine the coconut with the water in a small saucepan; bring the liquid to a boil. Reduce the heat; simmer 15 minutes. Place a small sieve over a small bowl; strain the coconut mixture. Reserve the liquid; discard the solids. Return the liquid to the saucepan; reduce to 1 cup. Stir in the cream. Set aside.

Heat ½ tablespoon of the oil in a 10-inch skillet. Add the shallots, garlic, and chile; cook over medium heat until the shallots are soft and transparent, 2 to 3 minutes.

Meanwhile, heat the remaining 1 tablespoon of oil in a 12-inch skillet. Add the shrimp; cook over high heat until they turn pink, 3 to 4 minutes. Add the shallot mixture to the shrimp; mix well. Add the coconut liquid to the shrimp, and continue cooking over high heat until the sauce reduces by one-third, about 4 minutes. Add the jícama, parsley, and lime juice to the shrimp; mix well and remove from the heat immediately. Garnish with the toasted coconut and serve.

---

*To toast coconut, spread it out on baking pan and bake in preheated 350°F oven for about 7 minutes, stirring once.

Sautéed Shrimp Diablo

▽▽▽▽▽▽▽▽▽▽▽▽▽▽▽▽▽▽

Serves 4

Shrimp Diablo means "shrimp the Devil's way" or, in other words, hot! These are really spicy, flavorful shrimp. If you want them to taste of the inferno, add more chile to the sauce as you cook it. Be careful not to overcook the sauce, it is supposed to be rich and chunky.

    2 tablespoons olive oil
    2 tablespoons minced shallots
    2 teaspoons minced garlic
    $\frac{1}{4}$ teaspoon crushed red pepper flakes
    32 large shrimp (about $1\frac{1}{2}$ pounds), peeled and deveined
    1 cup Fresh Tomato Sauce (page 61)
    1 cup Salsa Fresca (page 53)
    $\frac{3}{4}$ cup roasted cashews
    2 tablespoons chopped fresh cilantro

Heat the oil in a 12-inch skillet. Add the shallots, garlic, red pepper flakes, and shrimp; cook over medium heat until the shrimp begins to turn pink, about 3 minutes.

Add the Fresh Tomato Sauce to the shrimp mixture; cook until the sauce begins to simmer, about 1 minute. Add the Salsa Fresca, nuts, and cilantro; mix well. Remove from the heat. Serve immediately, spooning any extra sauce over the shrimp.

Grilled Flank Steak with Chipotle Chile Butter

▽▽▽▽▽▽▽▽▽▽▽▽▽▽▽▽▽▽

Serves 4

    1 tablespoon freshly squeezed lemon juice
    2 tablespoons olive oil
    4 (8-ounce) flank steaks, $\frac{3}{4}$ inch thick
    1 teaspoon freshly ground black pepper
    4 tablespoons Chipotle Chile Butter (page 55)

Preheat the broiler. Spray the broiler pan rack with nonstick cooking spray.

Mix the juice and oil in a small, shallow bowl. Coat each steak with the lemon mixture. Sprinkle pepper on each steak.

Place the steaks on the prepared rack; broil 4 inches from the heat, turning once, until cooked to the desired doneness: 4 minutes for rare, 6 minutes for medium rare, 8 minutes for medium, and 11 minutes for well done.

Garnish each steak with 1 tablespoon Chipotle Chile Butter.

NOTE

These steaks can also be prepared in a 12-inch skillet. Cook over medium-high heat, turning once, for the same desired doneness as the broiling time.

Grilled Chicken Breast Criollo with Mango Salsa

▽▽▽▽▽▽▽▽▽▽▽▽▽▽▽

Serves 4

This makes great grilling, and topped with Mango Salsa, it's quite a hit! Leftovers can be shredded and used in tacos and enchiladas and as a filling for Tostaditas (page 84).

- 1 cup Criollo Marinade (page 64)
- 4 (7-ounce) boneless skinless chicken breasts, pounded to a ¼-inch thickness
- 1 tablespoon peanut oil
- Mango Salsa (page 53)

Pour the marinade into a sealable plastic bag or nonreactive bowl; add the chicken. Seal or cover and refrigerate 2 hours.

Remove the chicken from the marinade. Heat the oil in a 12-inch skillet. Add the chicken and cook over medium heat, turning once, until browned and the juices run clear, about 6 minutes. Garnish with 4 tablespoons Mango Salsa per chicken breast.

Coconut Pecan Chicken

▽▽▽▽▽▽▽▽▽▽▽▽▽▽▽

Serves 4

This is a real favorite—a nutty, toasted coconut crust surrounding a tender, juicy chicken breast, topped with the lightly sweet taste of Mango Butter—it's irresistible!

- 8 skinless, boneless chicken breast halves
- 2 eggs
- 1 tablespoon water
- 1 teaspoon salt
- ½ teaspoon freshly ground pepper
- 1 cup pecans
- 1 cup shredded sweetened coconut
- 2 tablespoons olive oil
- 4 tablespoons Mango Butter (page 58)

Place the chicken breasts between two sheets of plastic wrap and lightly pound them with a small mallet to a ¼-inch thickness.

Beat the eggs with the water, salt, and pepper in a shallow bowl. Set aside.

Place the pecans in a food processor or blender; pulse the machine two to three times to lightly chop the nuts. Add the coconut to the pecans; pulse five to six times until crumbly and well combined (but not a paste). Transfer the pecan mixture to a sheet of waxed paper or a plate.

Dip the chicken in the egg mixture, then dredge in the pecan mixture, coating both sides well.

Heat the oil in a 12-inch skillet. Add the chicken. Cook over medium-low heat, turning once, until golden brown, about 8 minutes. Top each breast with ½ tablespoon of Mango Butter. Serve immediately.

Sugar Reef Chicken

Serves 8

This dish is sweet, spicy, and tangy all at the same time, but not overwhelmingly so. Barbecued or grilled, the chicken is tender and flavorful and makes a great company dish. Serve it over a bed of Costa Rican Rice (page 103) accompanied by sautéed vegetables, or try it with tortillas and your favorite salsa. Take this chicken on your next picnic.

1 quart + ½ cup water

½ tablespoon + 1 teaspoon Jamaican Jerk Spices, wet or dry (page 62)

1 tablespoon chopped fresh ginger root

1 tablespoon chopped garlic

1 cup unsweetened pineapple juice

1 cup peanut or vegetable oil

16 chicken thighs or breast halves (about 4 pounds)

7 tablespoons tamarind paste or mango chutney (page 151)

7 tablespoons light corn syrup

6 tablespoons + 2 teaspoons cider vinegar

8 tablespoons light molasses

1 teaspoon habanero hot sauce (or other hot sauce)

To make the marinade: Combine 1 quart of the water with ½ tablespoon of the Jamaican Jerk Spices, the ginger, and the garlic in a large saucepan. Cook over medium heat until the liquid begins to simmer. Remove from the heat; cool. Add the juice and oil to the cooled liquid; mix well.

Transfer the marinade to a nonreactive bowl or large sealable plastic bag; add the chicken. Cover or seal and refrigerate for 4 hours.

To make the glaze: Place the remaining ingredients in a food processor or blender; purée until smooth.

To bake: Preheat the oven to 350°F. Remove the chicken from the marinade; discard the marinade. Place the chicken in a large, shallow baking dish.

Bake the chicken, brushing on the glaze after the chicken has begun to brown, until the juices run clear and a meat thermometer placed in the center of the thickest pieces, not touching bone, registers 180°F, 30 to 40 minutes. Serve immediately.

To grill: Before starting, review "Barbecuing" on page 42. Barbecue the chicken, turning once, for 10 to 20 minutes, depending on the size of the piece. Generously brush on the glaze after the chicken has begun to brown.

Jamaican-Style BBQ Chicken Breasts with Pineapple Salsa

Serves 4

This dish combines the Caribbean flavors of jerk seasoning and fresh pineapple. It's a knockout dish!

4 chicken breasts, with skin
2 tablespoons + 2 teaspoons peanut oil
2 tablespoons dry Jamaican Jerk Spices
   (pages 62)

Pineapple Salsa

1 cup diced fresh pineapple
$\frac{1}{2}$ cup diced jícama
$\frac{1}{2}$ cup diced tomato
1 serrano or jalapeño chile, minced
$\frac{1}{4}$ cup diced red bell pepper
2 tablespoons freshly squeezed lime juice
2 tablespoons chopped fresh cilantro
Salt and freshly ground black pepper
   to taste

To prepare the chicken, rub the chicken with 2 tablespoons of the oil. Sprinkle the Jamaican Jerk Spices over both sides of the chicken; lightly rub it into the meat and skin. Place the chicken in a plastic bag or sealable container; refrigerate 4 hours.

Meanwhile, combine the salsa ingredients together in a nonreactive bowl; cover and refrigerate.

Heat the remaining 2 teaspoons of oil in a 12-inch skillet. Add the chicken; cook over high heat, skin side down, until the skin begins to crackle and crisp, about 3½ minutes. Lower the heat to medium, turn the chicken, and continue cooking until the juices run clear when cut in the thickest part of the breast, about 5 minutes.

Serve the chicken garnished with 2 or 3 tablespoons of the Pineapple Salsa.

To grill: Review "Barbecuing" on page 42. Cook the chicken on the grill, skin side down, until the skin becomes crisp and brown, 3 to 4 minutes. Turn the chicken and move it to a cooler part of the grill; continue cooking until the juices run clear when cut in the thickest part of the breast, about 5 to 7 minutes.

To broil: Preheat the broiler. Place the chicken in a shallow roasting pan; broil the chicken 4 to 6 inches from the heating element, skin side up, until the skin becomes crisp, about 6 minutes. Turn the chicken and continue to cook for 5 to 6 minutes. Turn the oven from broil to bake and continue cooking at 350°F until the juices run clear when cut in the thickest part of the breast, about 5 minutes.

Mayan Clay Pot Chicken

Serves 3 to 4

This is a savory, country-style way to prepare chicken. Serve the chicken topped with the savory clay pot juices accompanied by rice or potatoes.

1 (3½- to 4-pound) broiler chicken
4 tablespoons achiote paste (page 149)
½ cup freshly squeezed Seville orange juice (page 151)
½ medium red onion, sliced
6 garlic cloves, halved
1 jalapeño chile, sliced
1 red bell pepper, sliced
4 leafy sprigs of fresh spearmint
½ teaspoon freshly ground black pepper
½ teaspoon salt

Preheat the oven to 350°F. Soak the clay pot in water for 10 minutes. Drain.

Rinse the chicken in cool water; pat dry with paper towels. Dissolve the achiote paste in the juice; brush the mixture on the chicken.

Combine the onion, garlic, jalapeño chile, bell pepper, and mint in a medium-size bowl; mix well. Place three-quarters of this mixture into the bottom of the prepared clay pot. Place the remaining vegetable mixture into the cavity of the chicken. Place the chicken into the clay pot, breast side up, and cover with the remaining achiote mixture. Season with salt and pepper.

Cover the clay pot and bake until a meat thermometer (when placed into the center of the thickest part, but not touching bone) registers 180°F, about 1 hour 15 minutes.

Remove the pot from the oven; let stand 10 minutes. Remove the chicken from the pot; carve. Pour the liquid from the pot into a cup; skim off any fat. Serve as gravy for the chicken.

Clay Pot Cooking

Clay pot cooking is an ancient technique. Baking meats in the lidded pot creates the benefits of pit cooking—the cooking juices are sealed in to keep the meat moist and tender. Clay cooking pots can be found in the cookware section of major department stores, in cookware specialty stores, and through cookware mail-order catalogs. If you don't have a clay pot, use a heavy, lidded casserole.

Apple-Roasted Duck with Apple-Jalapeño Chutney

Serves 4

This is a knockout dish: The chutney is spicy sweet with a bite and complements the flavor of the roasted meat. Instead of duck, try this with a capon or even a pork loin (split it and stuff it)—the results will be equally delicious.

4 Granny Smith apples, cored and
  quartered

1 medium onion, quartered

2 jalapeño chiles

1/4 pineapple, cubed (about 1 1/2 cups)

1/2 cup freshly squeezed lemon juice

1 teaspoon ground cinnamon

1 teaspoon freshly ground black pepper

Two 4-pound ducks, split, with skin on
  and fat removed

Apple-Jalapeño Chutney (below)

Preheat the oven to 350°F. Combine the apples, onion, chiles, pineapple, lemon juice, cinnamon, and pepper in a food processor or blender; purée until smooth. Rub the apple mixture under the skin and inside the cavities of the ducks.

Place ducks, breast side up, in a shallow roasting pan. Cover and roast 30 minutes. Uncover the ducks and continue roasting until the skin becomes crispy and golden brown, about 30 minutes more.

Remove the birds from the oven. Carve the ducks, placing 1 thigh and 1 duck half on each plate. Top with warm Apple-Jalapeño Chutney and serve.

---

*The zest of the lemon is the outermost peel of the fruit without any of the pith (white membrane). To remove the zest, use a zester or the fine side of a vegetable grater.

Apple-Jalapeño Chutney

4 Granny Smith or Pippin apples, cored
  and cut into 1/2-inch cubes

2 jalapeño chiles, thinly sliced

1 medium onion, diced into 1/2-inch cubes

1/2 red bell pepper, diced

1/2 cup golden raisins

1 cup fresh or frozen cranberries

2 1/2 tablespoons fresh cilantro, chopped

1 tablespoon lemon zest*

2 tablespoons freshly squeezed lemon
  juice

1/2 cup honey

1/2 cup apple cider vinegar

1/4 cup packed dark brown sugar

1/2 tablespoon ground cinnamon

1/4 teaspoon freshly grated nutmeg

1/2 teaspoon chopped ginger root

Combine all the ingredients in a large saucepan. Bring the mixture to a boil. Reduce the heat to low, stir, and cover. Simmer until the apple skins begin to turn pale, about 20 minutes. Remove from the heat. Serve warm.

Defatting a Duck

To remove the fat from a duck, prick the breasts with a fork four or five times. Parboil the bird for 3 minutes; then take the duck from the water and let cool. Pick out the remaining fat deposits. This won't be difficult, because the parboiling will make the fat deposits very easy to see.

Turkey Yucateca

Serves 10 to 12

This is a bird you won't forget. The meat is juicy and tender, the dressing is sweet, fruity, and spicy with the combined flavors of tropical fruits, liqueur, and the smoky bite of chipotle chiles and achiote. The sauce is fantastic! You'll need a cooking bag, which can be found in any supermarket in the plastic-wrap section, to prepare this dish. The bag makes the turkey extra-moist and cleanup a snap!

3 Granny Smith or Pippin apples (about 1 pound), cored and chopped, with peels left on

1½ pounds dried fruit mix (apricot, mango, pineapple, and papaya)

½ cup frozen orange juice concentrate

½ cup pineapple juice

½ cup chipotle chiles en adobo (canned smoked jalapeño chiles)

1 cup tequila or rum

1 cup orange liqueur

5 tablespoons butter, softened

1 (10- to 12-pound) young fresh tom turkey

2 tablespoons salt

2 tablespoons freshly ground black pepper

2 tablespoons achiote paste (page 149)

2 tablespoons minced garlic

In a medium-size bowl, combine the apples, dried fruits, orange juice concentrate, and pineapple juice. Set aside.

In Praise of the Cooking Bag

Use a cooking bag to save on cleanup and keep your bird constantly basted in the cooking juices. This is effortless cooking: Put the stuffed turkey in a preheated oven and go about your daily routine. Open the oven door a few hours later, and you've got a tender, juicy bird ready for your table.

Combine the chiles, tequila, and orange liqueur in a food processor or blender; purée until it becomes a liquid paste. Pour the liquid over the apple mixture; let sit for 30 minutes.

Place a small sieve over a small bowl. Strain the fruit mixture; reserve both the liquid and the solids. Add 2½ tablespoons of the butter to the fruit mixture. Set aside.

Preheat the oven to 350°F. Rinse the turkey inside and out, and pat it dry with paper towels. Combine the salt, pepper, achiote paste, and garlic in a small bowl; mix well. Rub the body and cavity of the turkey with the salt mixture.

Press 3 cups of the solid fruit mixture into the body cavity of the turkey and 2 cups into the front cavity (wishbone area). Insert a cooking thermometer into the thickest part of the breast, not touching the bone.

Place the turkey into a cooking bag, breast side up; pour the reserved liquid and remaining fruit mixture over the turkey. Seal the bag, gathering it on top to form a natural "chimney." Place bagged turkey into a large roasting pan, making sure the bag is not hanging over the sides.

Bake the turkey until the meat thermometer registers 180°F, about 3 hours.

Remove the turkey from the oven; let it rest for 45 to 60 minutes. Remove the fruit mixture from the cavities. Pour the sauce into a cup and skim off any excess fat. Serve the carved turkey with the fruit dressing and sauce.

Place the turkey in the cooking bag so that the bag will close on top to form a "chimney."

Rasta Pasta with Calypso Salsa

Serves 4

This is a tasty, vegetarian pasta dish. For variety, top each serving with Chicken Breast Criollo (page 121) and a heaping spoonful of Mango Salsa (page 53).

> 1 cup shredded sweetened coconut
> 1½ cups water
> 1½ pounds fresh fettuccine
> 4 tablespoons olive oil
> 2 teaspoons minced garlic
> 4 teaspoons minced shallots
> ⅛ teaspoon crushed red pepper flakes
> ½ cup heavy cream
> 8 tablespoons freshly grated Parmesan cheese
> 2 teaspoons chopped fresh parsley
> Calypso Salsa (page 52)

Combine the coconut and water in a small saucepan; bring the liquid to a boil. Reduce the heat; simmer 5 minutes. Place a small sieve over a small bowl. Strain the coconut mixture. Reserve the liquid; discard the solids. Set aside.

Cook the pasta according to the package's directions for *al dente*. Toss the cooked, drained pasta with 2 tablespoons of the oil in a large bowl. Set aside.

Heat the remaining 2 tablespoons of oil in a 12-inch skillet. Add the garlic, shallots, and red pepper flakes; cook over medium heat until the shallots are transparent, about 2 minutes. Add the pasta mixture, coconut liquid, and cream to the garlic mixture. Simmer, stirring occasionally, until the pasta absorbs the liquid, 3 to 4 minutes. Add the cheese and parsley; toss well. Serve immediately, topped with Calypso Salsa.

Fettuccine with Shiitake Mushrooms and Fresh Tomato Sauce

Serves 4

This is a great vegetarian entrée.

- 1½ pounds fresh fettuccine
- 4 tablespoons olive oil
- 2 tablespoons minced shallots
- 4 teaspoons minced garlic
- 3 cups shiitake mushrooms, sliced
- 2 cups Fresh Tomato Sauce (page 61)
- 1 cup diced tomatoes
- 1 teaspoon salt
- ¼ teaspoon freshly ground black pepper
- 2 teaspoons minced fresh parsley
- 4 rounded tablespoons freshly grated Parmesan cheese
- ½ cup Salsa Fresca (page 53)

Cook the fettuccine according to the package's directions for *al dente*. Toss the cooked, drained pasta with 2 tablespoons of the oil in a large bowl. Keep warm.

Meanwhile, heat the remaining 2 tablespoons of oil in a 12-inch skillet. Add the shallots, garlic, and mushrooms; cook over medium heat, stirring frequently, until the mushrooms soften, 3 to 4 minutes. Add the Fresh Tomato Sauce, tomatoes, salt, pepper, parsley, and 2 tablespoons of the cheese. Cook until heated through.

Add the tomato sauce mixture to the pasta; toss. Serve immediately. Garnish with Salsa Fresca and the remaining cheese.

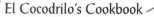

SPIDER MONKEYS

Spider monkeys—like all New World monkeys—have prehensile tails that they use as extra arms. This fifth limb helps them swing effortlessly through the forest canopy as they search for fruit. A pad of "nonskid" skin at the tip of their tails improves their grip, allowing the monkeys to use their tails to grasp objects, hang from tree branches, hold an infant, explore tree crevices, and brush away insects. The tails also help them balance as they leap from tree to tree. Hanging by their tails with all other limbs free, the acrobatic monkeys resemble spiders suspended from their webs.

Long, muscular arms and legs and light, slender bodies enable these monkeys to move easily through the canopy. Restless and agile, the spider monkeys move like trapeze artists, leaping or dropping twenty-five feet at a time through the tops of trees as high as one hundred feet above the forest floor.

High in the canopy, the monkeys eat, sleep, and raise their young. Spider monkeys feed solely on fruit, yet are surprisingly finicky eaters. They sniff fruit to see if it is ripe, and they will drop the fruit to the ground after a bite if it is not to their taste. These monkeys live in groups, often helping each other with child care, grooming each other, chattering together, and standing guard. They sleep in large troops, sometimes made up of one hundred individuals, but they break up into smaller bands during the day. The usual social grouping consists of females tending to their young, and sometimes one adult male. Males, who are dominant to females, often wander by themselves. Baby monkeys cling to the fur on their mother's belly but soon learn to ride on their mothers' backs or take off on their own for a swing through the trees.

Spider monkeys are gentle, unaggressive animals and there are few fights within their groups. When males are present in the group, they threaten intruders with barks or by defecating; sometimes they break branches and drop them onto the intruder. The spider monkeys' natural enemies are hawks and eagles, since they are among the few rain forest dwellers who have access to the lofty world of the spider monkey.

Iguana iguana

DESSERTS

Inca Nut Torte

Makes one 10-inch torte

This is a very rich white chocolate brownie—dense and chewy. The hidden bit of chile adds a barely perceptible zing to the chocolaty treat. Serve with a dollop of fresh whipped cream, chopped Brazil nuts, and a sprig of mint. To serve the torte warm, microwave each portion on Medium 20 seconds, then garnish.

¼ cup graham cracker crumbs

1 pound white chocolate, shaved or cut into small pieces

3 eggs

½ teaspoon vanilla

¼ teaspoon crushed red pepper flakes

¾ cup light corn syrup

¼ cup butter, melted

½ cup chopped Brazil nuts

½ cups chopped cashews

Preheat the oven to 280°F. Grease a 10-inch springform pan. Sprinkle the graham cracker crumbs in the pan. Tap the pan, making the crumbs stick to the bottom and side; discard the excess crumbs.

Melt the chocolate in the top of a double-boiler over medium heat, stirring often. Set aside.

Combine the eggs, vanilla, red pepper flakes, and corn syrup in a small bowl; beat together. Add the chocolate, butter, and nuts to the egg mixture; mix well.

Pour the batter into the prepared pan. Bake until golden brown and the sides pull away from the pan, about 1 hour 15 minutes. Let stand for 1½ hours; remove the side from the pan. Chill before serving.

Jamaican Bread Pudding

Makes 12 puddings

Garnish these individual puddings with confectioner's sugar, drizzles of raspberry Melba sauce, fruit syrup, or Passionfruit Glaze (page 150), or Apricot-Lime Glaze (page 138).

½ cup raisins

4 tablespoons rum

3 eggs

1 cup sugar

1 teaspoon vanilla

Pinch of freshly grated nutmeg

2 cups whole milk

¼ cup butter, melted

4 cups cubed bread (½-inch cubes)

1½ cups diced fresh fruit or fruit cocktail (oranges, mangos, cherries, pineapple), drained (do not use bananas)

Preheat the oven to 325°F. Grease 12 muffin cups well.

Combine the raisins and rum in a small microwavable bowl; microwave on high for 20 seconds. Set aside.

Cream the eggs and sugar in a large bowl. Add the vanilla, nutmeg, and milk; mix well. Add the melted butter to the milk mixture; mix well.

Combine the bread and raisin mixture in a large bowl; mix well. Add the bread mixture to the milk mixture; mix well. Stir in the mixed fruit; mix gently (do not mash the fruit).

Divide the batter evenly among the muffin cups. Bake until golden brown, 35 to 40 minutes. Garnish, if desired; serve warm.

Caribbean-Style Rice Pudding

Serves 6

For an elegant presentation, serve this pudding in Buttercrunch Cookie Baskets (page 136) topped with a dollop of whipped cream and a sprinkle of cinnamon.

- 1 cup long grain white rice
- 1¼ cups whole milk
- ⅓ cup *cajeta* or sweetened condensed milk
- 1 cup sugar
- ½ stick cinnamon, crushed (about ½ tablespoon)
- 1 teaspoon lemon zest*
- ½ teaspoon vanilla
- Whipped Cream, to garnish
- Cinnamon, to garnish

Bring 6 cups of water to a boil in a medium saucepan. Add the rice. Simmer until tender and the grains are split, 35 to 40 minutes. Drain.

Transfer the drained rice to a medium saucepan; add the remaining ingredients. Cook over low heat until the mixture is thick, 15 to 20 minutes. Remove from the heat.

Divide the mixture among 6 individual serving dishes; serve warm or refrigerate until chilled. Garnish with whipped cream and a dash of cinnamon.

*The zest of the lemon is the outermost peel of the fruit without any of the pith (white membrane). To remove the zest, use a zester or the fine side of a vegetable grater.

Aruba Lime Fruit Bowl

Makes 8 servings

- 1 cup diced fruit (melon, mangos, and papayas, or berries and other fresh fruits)
- Juice of ½ lime
- 1 teaspoon sugar
- 1 cup whipping cream
- 8 Buttercrunch Cookie Baskets (page 136)
- 4 cups Key Lime Pie filling (page 137), chilled
- 8 sprigs of fresh mint for garnish

In a small bowl, mix the fruit with the juice and sugar. In a medium-size bowl, whip the cream until soft peaks form.

Fill each Buttercrunch Cookie Basket with Key Lime Pie filling. Top each basket with 2 tablespoons of the fruit mixture. Garnish each with a dollop of whipped cream and a sprig of mint. Serve immediately.

Cajeta

Cajeta is sweetened caramelized goat's milk, which is sold in jars in Latin groceries. If unavailable, substitute sweetened condensed milk.

Chocolate Brazil Nut Pie

Save the Rain Forest Pie

Makes two 9-inch pies

Pie Crust (below)
4 tablespoons butter
3 eggs
2 cups coarsely chopped Brazil nuts
1 cup sugar
1 cup light corn syrup
2 teaspoons vanilla
Chocolate Truffle Topping (below)

Prepare the Pie Crust. Preheat the oven to 350°F.

Combine the butter, eggs, nuts, sugar, corn syrup, and vanilla in a medium-size bowl; blend well. Pour the filling into the Pie Crust. Bake until firm, about 40 minutes. Chill. Top with Chocolate Truffle Topping.

Pie Crust

1 cup all-purpose flour
Pinch of salt
6 tablespoons vegetable shortening
1/3 to 1/2 cup cold water

Combine the flour and salt in a small bowl. Cut the shortening into the flour mixture until the mixture is crumbly. Add the water, 1 tablespoon at a time, until the dough just holds together.

Gather the pastry into a ball; chill for 30 minutes. Cut the dough in half; roll each half out onto a lightly floured board. Fit each half into a 9-inch pie pan; refrigerate the pie crusts.

Chocolate Truffle Topping

1/4 cup heavy cream
1 1/4 cups shaved semisweet chocolate, about 6 ounces
6 tablespoons butter, softened and cut into small pieces
2 tablespoons raspberry Melba sauce or seedless raspberry jam
2 tablespoons triple sec liqueur
Shavings of white chocolate, optional

Slowly warm the cream in a saucepan over low heat or in the top of a double boiler over simmering water, until it reaches 180°F on a candy thermometer. **Do not let the cream boil.** Remove from the heat; cool to 120°F, about 3 minutes. Add the semisweet chocolate, a little at a time, stirring constantly, until the chocolate is melted and the mixture is well blended. Slowly blend in the butter. Add the sauce and liqueur; mix well. Spread the chocolate mixture evenly over both cooled pies. Garnish with white chocolate, if desired.

Cutting In

The process of cutting in is the mixing of a solid fat (such as butter or shortening) with a dry ingredient (such as flour) until the mixture forms small particles. Using a fork, press the shortening into the flour, continuing cutting until the mixture forms coarse little grains. Cutting in can also be accomplished by using a tool called a pastry blender, two knives, and even your fingertips (if you make sure your hands are cool and you don't handle the dough so much that the fat melts). A food processor can also be used, just be careful not to overwork the ingredients and make a paste. A few short pulses should do the trick

Buttercrunch Cookie Baskets

Makes 8

These crunchy baskets make elegant and tasty containers for Key Lime Pie filling (page 137), The Crocodile's Dream (page 144), and Caribbean-Style Rice Pudding (page 134). Or use them for serving ice cream or sorbets.

- ½ cup butter, softened
- ½ cup light corn syrup
- ⅔ cup packed dark brown sugar
- 1 cup old-fashioned oats
- ¾ cup all-purpose flour
- 1 teaspoon vanilla

Preheat the oven to 375°F. Line baking sheets with parchment paper or use nonstick baking sheets.

Combine the butter, corn syrup, and brown sugar in a medium saucepan; cook over medium heat, stirring constantly, until the sugar dissolves, 4 to 5 minutes. Increase the heat and bring the mixture to a boil; remove from the heat. Stir in the oats, flour, and vanilla. Mix well.

Drop 1 tablespoon of dough onto each end of the prepared baking sheet (bake only 2 baskets per sheet). Bake until the dough becomes bubbly, spreads, and begins to turn a rich brown, about 12 minutes.

Remove from the oven; let stand for about 1 minute. Remove the baskets with a spatula and let them cool over inverted custard cups. Remove the baskets from the cups when cooled; store in an airtight container.

After letting the cookies cool for about 1 minute, drape each one over an inverted custard cup.

Key Lime Pie

Makes two 9-inch pies

This sweet-tart pie is fantastic by itself and the perfect end note to a seafood dinner. It is imperative that the lime juice you use in this recipe be fresh; don't be tempted to use bottled lime juice. Mini-food processors, with the right attachments, make quick work of juicing fresh limes.

> Graham Cracker Crust (below)
> Two 14-ounce cans sweetened condensed milk
> 8 egg yolks
> 1 cup fresh Florida Key lime juice
> Zest from 4 limes*
> Whipped Topping (below)

Preheat the oven to 350°F. Prepare and bake the Graham Cracker Crust as directed.

Combine the milk and egg yolks in a medium-size bowl; mix well. Add the juice and zest; blend well. Pour the pie filling into two cooled pie shells. Bake until set, about 12 minutes. Allow the pies to cool before adding the Whipped Topping.

Graham Cracker Crust

> 2½ cups graham cracker crumbs
> 6 tablespoons sugar
> 8 tablespoons butter, melted
> 1 teaspoon ground cinnamon

Preheat the oven to 350°F.

Combine all the ingredients in a medium-size bowl; mix well. Press the mixture into two 9-inch pie plates. Bake 12 minutes; set aside to cool.

---

*The zest of the lemon is the outermost peel of the fruit without any of the pith (white membrane). To remove the zest, use a zester or the fine side of a vegetable grater.

Whipped Topping

> 2 cups whipping cream
> 6 tablespoons sugar
> Fresh mint, for garnish
> Lime, thinly sliced, for garnish

Whip the cream and sugar together in a small bowl until soft peaks form. Top the cooled pies with the cream mixture. Garnish each pie with a mint leaf or slices of lime.

Key Lime Meringue Pie

If you prefer, use the leftover egg whites to make a meringue to top the pies instead of the whipped cream.

> 5 egg whites
> ½ cup sugar

Place the egg whites a medium-size, clean, dry bowl. Whip the egg whites until they begin to get frothy. Slowly add the sugar, 1 tablespoon at a time, until the mixture forms stiff white peaks. Spread the meringue over the cooled pies.

To lightly brown the peaks, place the pie under the broiler for 1 minute. Watch carefully to avoid burning.

Key Limes

Key limes are different from the common green lime found readily in the supermarket. Key limes are smaller and more yellow. Since they are almost impossible to find outside their native Florida, regular limes can be substituted.

Mango Cheesecake

Makes one 10-inch cake

For a nice tangy complement, serve individual slices of Mango Cheesecake garnished with a drizzle of Passionfruit Glaze (page 150) or Apricot-Lime Glaze (see note this page).

> Graham Cracker Crust (below)
> Two 8-ounce packages cream cheese, at room temperature
> 1 cup sugar
> 1½ cups sour cream
> 3 eggs
> 1½ cups mango purée (made from fresh or frozen thawed mangos)
> ½ teaspoon vanilla
> 1 teaspoon freshly squeezed lemon juice
> Sour Cream Topping

Preheat the oven 300°F. Prepare the Graham Cracker Crust, as directed.

Combine the cream cheese and sugar in a food processor or blender; blend until the sugar dissolves. Slowly add the sour cream, eggs, mango purée, vanilla, and juice; blend well. Pour the mixture into the prepared crust. Bake until set, 1 hour.

Remove the cake from the oven; raise the temperature to 350°F. Let the cake cool to room temperature. Top with the Sour Cream Topping. Return the cake to the oven; bake 4 minutes. Chill for at least 4 hours.

Graham Cracker Crust

> 1¼ cup graham cracker crumbs
> ¼ cup ground roasted cashews
> ¼ cup sugar
> 3 tablespoons butter, melted

Combine the graham cracker crumbs, cashews, and sugar in a small bowl; mix to combine. Add the butter; mix well. Press into the bottom of a 10-inch springform pan.

Sour Cream Topping

> 1½ cups sour cream
> ½ cup sugar

Combine the sour cream and sugar in a food processor or blender; blend well.

If you cannot find passionfruit glaze in your supermarket, use this Apricot-Lime Glaze. Purée 2 tablespoons apricot jam, 2 tablespoons corn syrup, 1 teaspoon freshly squeezed lime juice, and 1 teaspoon cider vinegar in a food processor or blender. This makes approximately ⅓ cup.

Yonis's Lemon Cheesecake

Makes one 10-inch cake

Graham Cracker Crust (below)

Two 8-ounce packages cream cheese, at
  room temperature

1 cup sugar

3 eggs

$1\frac{1}{2}$ cups sour cream

3 drops vanilla

$\frac{1}{4}$ cup freshly squeezed lemon juice

Zest of 2 lemons*

Sour Cream Topping (below)

1 lemon, thinly sliced for garnish

Preheat the oven to 300°F. Prepare the Graham
Cracker Crust, as directed.

Combine the cream cheese and sugar in a food
processor or blender; blend until well combined.
Add the eggs, one at a time, mixing well after
each addition. Add the sour cream, vanilla, juice,
and zest, in that order, to the cheese mixture.
Pour the mixture into the prepared crust.

Bake 50 to 60 minutes. If the cake is not set by
then, reduce the heat to 250°F; bake 10 minutes
more. Remove from the oven; let cool to room
temperature. Top with the Sour Cream Topping.
Chill for at least 4 hours. Garnish with thinly
sliced lemon before serving.

Graham Cracker Crust

3 tablespoons butter, melted

1 cup graham cracker crumbs

$\frac{1}{4}$ cup ground cashews

2 tablespoons sugar

Grease the sides of one 10-inch springform pan.

Combine all the ingredients in a small bowl; mix
well. Press into the bottom and sides of the pan.

Sour Cream Topping

$1\frac{3}{4}$ cups sour cream

Zest of 1 lemon*

$\frac{1}{2}$ cup sugar

Combine the sour cream and zest in a food processor or blender; blend well. Add the sugar; mix
thoroughly.

*The zest of the lemon is the outermost peel of the
fruit without any of the pith (white membrane). To
remove the zest, use a zester or the fine side of a
vegetable grater.

Yonis's Banana Cheesecake

Makes one 10-inch cake

Graham Cracker Crust (below)
Two 8-ounce packages cream cheese, at
   room temperature
1 cup sugar
3 eggs
$\frac{1}{2}$ pound ripe bananas, puréed
$1\frac{1}{2}$ cups sour cream
1 teaspoon vanilla
2 tablespoons finely chopped cashews
Sour Cream Topping (below)

Preheat the oven to 300°F. Prepare the Graham Cracker Crust.

Combine the cream cheese and sugar in a food processor or blender; blend until well combined. Add the eggs, one at a time, mixing well after each addition. Add the bananas, sour cream, and vanilla, in that order, to the cheese mixture. Pour the mixture into the prepared crust.

Bake until set, 50 to 60 minutes. If the cake is not set by then, reduce the heat to 250°F; bake 10 minutes more. Remove from the oven; raise the temperature to 350°F. Let the cake cool to room temperature. Top with Sour Cream Topping. Return the cake to the oven; bake 4 minutes. Chill for at least 4 hours.

Sour Cream Topping

$1\frac{3}{4}$ cups sour cream
$\frac{1}{2}$ cup sugar

Combine the sour cream and sugar in a food processor or blender; blend well.

Graham Cracker Crust

$1\frac{1}{4}$ cup graham cracker crumbs
$\frac{1}{4}$ cup ground cashews
3 tablespoons melted butter
2 tablespoons sugar

Grease the sides of one 10-inch springform pan.

Mix all the ingredients in a small bowl. Press into the bottom and side of the pan.

Chocolate Lover's Crust

Substitute $1\frac{1}{4}$ cups chocolate wafer cookie crumbs (cream filling removed) for the graham crackers, cashews, and sugar.

Mocha Cheesecake

Substitute 4 tablespoons coffee liqueur, 2 tablespoons brewed espresso, and $\frac{1}{4}$ cup shaved semisweet chocolate for the banana purée. Pour the filling into a Chocolate Lover's Crust (above). Garnish with shaved semisweet chocolate.

Pumpkin Cheesecake

Substitute 8 ounces pumpkin purée for the banana purée and $\frac{1}{8}$ teaspoon freshly grated nutmeg for the vanilla. Garnish with chopped pecans.

Chocolate Truffle Torte

Makes one 10-inch torte

This torte is a very elegant, rich dessert. It is the perfect ending for a luncheon or dinner.

Chocolate Pie Crust (right)

1 cup heavy cream

12 ounces shaved semisweet chocolate

10 tablespoons unsalted butter, at room temperature

$\frac{1}{4}$ cup raspberry Melba sauce or seedless raspberry jam

$\frac{1}{8}$ cup orange liqueur

$\frac{1}{8}$ cup raspberry liqueur

$\frac{1}{2}$ cup shaved white chocolate for garnish

Prepare the Chocolate Pie Crust.

Cook the cream in the top of a double boiler over simmering water, until it reaches 180°F on a candy thermometer. Remove from the heat; cool to 120°. Slowly add the semisweet chocolate, stirring constantly, until well blended. (If the mixture becomes lumpy, return the pan to the top of the double boiler over hot water, stirring constantly until smooth.) Add the butter, 1 piece at a time, blending it well into the cream mixture. Stir in the sauce and the liqueurs.

Pour the mixture into the prepared crust. Chill 1 hour. Garnish with the white chocolate.

Chocolate Pie Crust

1 cup crushed chocolate wafer cookies

2 tablespoons butter

$\frac{1}{2}$ cup crushed toasted almond slivers

Combine the cookie crumbs and butter in a small bowl; mix well. Add the almonds; mix. Press the mixture into the bottom and sides of one 10-inch springform pan.

Melba Sauce

Melba sauce is a combination of puréed and strained raspberries, red currant jelly, sugar, and cornstarch. It is used as the topping for desserts such as Peach Melba. Melba sauce, Peach Melba, and Melba toast were created by the famous nineteenth-century French chef Auguste Escoffier for the popular Australian opera singer Dame Nellie Melba. Melba sauce is available in specialty food stores.

Sammy's Ibarra Chocolate Cake

Makes one 9-inch layer cake

This rich, flavorful cake bakes up beautifully and makes a great presentation. It tastes good warm with just a scoop of vanilla ice cream. Or stack the layers and use a rich chocolate fudge frosting as a filling, topping the cake with Melba sauce and fresh whipped cream. Garnish it all with fresh raspberries—make it as decadent as possible.

3 pounds Ibarra chocolate (page 150), shaved or cut into small pieces

1 tablespoon ground cinnamon

2 cups sour cream

8 eggs

2 tablespoons vanilla

1 cup butter

4½ cups all-purpose flour

1 cup sugar

2 teaspoons baking powder

2 teaspoons baking soda

1 tablespoon salt

1½ cups heavy cream

2 cups sliced almonds (optional)

Ibarra is the brand name of a Mexican-style chocolate. It comes in 3-ounce cakes formed of cacao nibs, sugar, cinnamon, and almonds. Sold in boxes of six, it's available in some supermarkets, in Latin markets, and through mail order.

Preheat the oven to 325°F. Grease and flour two 9-inch cake pans or two 10-inch springform pans.

Melt the chocolate in the top a double boiler over simmering water. Don't let the temperature of the chocolate exceed 110°F on a candy thermometer.

Combine the cinnamon, sour cream, eggs, vanilla, and melted chocolate in a medium-size bowl; mix well. Beat in ½ cup of the butter.

Sift together the flour, sugar, baking powder, baking soda, and salt in a large bowl. Beat in the remaining ½ cup of butter. Add the chocolate mixture to the flour mixture; mix well. Add the cream and almonds; mix well.

Pour the batter evenly into the prepared pans. Bake until a toothpick inserted into the center comes out clean, about 1½ hours.

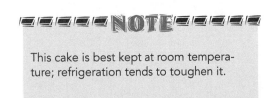

NOTE

This cake is best kept at room temperature; refrigeration tends to toughen it.

Aaron's Slightly More Sinful Flourless Ibarra Chocolate Cake

Makes one 10-inch layer cake

Frost and stack the cakes or serve them in small slices garnished with powdered sugar. These cakes are excellent topped with whipped cream and Ibarra chocolate shavings.

8 egg whites

¾ cup sugar

1 pound + 2 ounces Ibarra chocolate (page 150), shaved or cut into small pieces

½ pound unsalted butter

1 tablespoon freshly squeezed lemon juice

4 tablespoons orange liqueur

1 teaspoon vanilla

Adjust the oven rack to the lower third of the oven. Preheat the oven to 250°F. Grease and flour two 10-inch springform pans or two 9-inch cake pans.

Using a hand mixer or beater, whip the egg whites in a small bowl. When they begin to form small peaks, slowly add the sugar, a little at a time. Continue beating until the egg whites become stiff and glossy, about 7 minutes. Set aside.

Place the chocolate and butter in the top of a double boiler; melt over simmering water, stirring constantly.

Transfer the chocolate mixture to a large bowl. Add the juice; with a wire whisk beat until well combined. Add the liqueur, whisking to combine. Add the vanilla; beat together.

Gently fold the egg white mixture, one-quarter at a time, into the chocolate mixture. Pour the batter evenly into the prepared pans. Bake, on the lower rack, until a toothpick inserted into the center comes out clean, about 1½ hours. Cool the layers before removing them from the pans. Garnish with shaved chocolate.

The Crocodile's Dream

Serves 10 to 12

This dish is the essence of chocolate decadence. Use an ice cream scoop to spoon it from the baking pan, as its consistency is similar to a gooey brownie. Serve the scoops in Buttercrunch Cookie Baskets (page 136) and garnished with a dollop of fresh whipped cream, chopped cashew nuts, and a sprig of mint. It's wonderful served warm: Simply reheat it in the microwave for 20 seconds before putting it in the cookie basket; then garnish and serve.

  ¼ cup butter, softened
  1½ cups unsweetened cocoa powder
  1 cup sugar
  4 eggs
  1¾ cups light corn syrup
  2 teaspoons vanilla
  2 tablespoons cold brewed espresso
    coffee
  1 cup chopped Brazil nuts

Preheat the oven to 280°F. Generously grease a 9 x 13-inch baking dish.

Beat the butter, cocoa, and sugar in a large bowl. Stir in the eggs; blend well. Mix in the corn syrup. Combine the vanilla and espresso in a small bowl; add to the cocoa mixture and mix well. Stir in the Brazil nuts.

Pour the mixture into the prepared baking dish; bake until a toothpick inserted into the center comes out clean, about 1 hour 15 minutes. Cool 1 hour before serving.

Jefferson's Pecan Pie

Makes two 9-inch pies

  Pastry Shells (below)
  6 eggs
  2 cups light corn syrup
  1 teaspoon vanilla
  6 tablespoons butter, melted
  2 cups sugar
  3 cups pecan halves

Preheat the oven to 350°F. Prepare the Pastry Shells, as directed.

Combine the eggs, corn syrup, vanilla, butter, and sugar in a medium-size bowl; mix well. Set aside.

Spread one-half of the pecans evenly over the bottom of each prepared pie shell. Pour half of the egg mixture into each of the pie shells.

Bake until the crust is golden brown, about 50 minutes. Cool and serve.

Pastry Shells

  2½ cups all-purpose flour
  Pinch of salt
  ⅔ cup shortening
  ⅔ cup cold water

Combine the flour and salt in a small bowl. Cut the shortening into the flour mixture until the mixture is crumbly. Add the water, 1 tablespoon at a time, until the dough just holds together. Gather the pastry into a ball; chill for 30 minutes.

Cut the dough in half; roll each half out onto a lightly floured board. Fit the pastry into two 9-inch pie pans; refrigerate the prepared pie shells for 30 minutes.

Walnut Pie

Makes two 9-inch pies

Serve these pies warm or at room temperature. Place a scoop of vanilla ice cream alongside each slice.

Pie Shells (below)
2½ cups coarsely chopped walnuts
1½ cups granulated sugar
½ cup packed light brown sugar
6 eggs
2 teaspoons vanilla
4 tablespoons butter
2 cups dark corn syrup

Preheat the oven to 350°F. Prepare the Pie Shells.

Combine the walnuts, granulated sugar, brown sugar, eggs, vanilla, butter, and corn syrup in a medium bowl; mix well.

Pour half of the filling into each prepared pie shell. Bake until the crust is golden brown, 45 to 50 minutes. Cool slightly before serving.

Pie Shells

2½ cups all-purpose flour
Pinch of salt
⅔ cup shortening
⅔ cup cold water

Combine the flour and salt in a small bowl. Cut the shortening into the flour mixture until the mixture is crumbly. Add the water, 1 tablespoon at a time, until the dough just holds together. Gather the pastry into ball; chill for 30 minutes.

Cut the dough in half; roll each half out onto a lightly floured board. Fit the pastry into two 9-inch pie pans; refrigerate the prepared pie shells for 30 minutes.

The Fishwife's Pecan Pralines

Makes 18 candies

2½ cups sugar
1 teaspoon baking soda
⅛ teaspoon ground cinnamon
1 cup buttermilk
¼ cup butter
2 cups pecan halves

Place parchment or waxed paper over 2 baking sheets. Set aside.

Combine the sugar, baking soda, cinnamon, buttermilk, and butter in a large saucepan; cook over medium high heat, without stirring, until the mixture reaches 238°F on a candy thermometer (or when a small amount of this mixture dropped in very cold water forms a soft ball). Immediately remove from the heat. Stir in the pecans. With a wooden spoon, beat vigorously, until the mixture turns cloudy, about 1 minute.

Immediately drop the mixture by tablespoonfuls onto the prepared baking sheets to form 2- to 2½-inch diameter pralines. Cool until firm. Store in an airtight container.

Sun-dried Cranberry-Apple Pie

Makes two 9-inch pies

Sun-dried cranberries add a nice twist to apple pie. Serve this warm with a scoop of vanilla ice cream.

Pastry Shells (below)
1/2 cup sun-dried cranberries
10 Red Delicious apples, peeled, cored, and coarsely chopped
1/2 cup sugar
1/2 teaspoon ground cinnamon
Crumbly Topping (below)

Preheat oven to 350°F. Prepare the Pastry Shells, as directed.

Combine cranberries, apples, sugar and cinnamon in a large bowl; mix well. Place half of the filling evenly in each prepared pie shell. Sprinkle with Crumbly Topping. Bake until the crust is golden brown, 50 to 60 minutes.

Pastry Shells

2 cups all-purpose flour
4 tablespoons sugar
1/8 teaspoon salt
1 cup cold unsalted butter, cut into small pieces
6 tablespoons cold water

Combine the flour, sugar and salt in a small bowl. Cut the butter into the flour mixture until the mixture is crumbly. Add the water, 1 tablespoon at a time, until the dough just holds together. Gather the pastry into ball; chill for 30 minutes.

Cut the dough in half; roll each half out onto a lightly floured board. Fit the pastry into two 9-inch pie pans; refrigerate the prepared pie shells for 30 minutes.

Crumbly Topping

1/2 cup unsalted butter, cut into small pieces
1 cup all-purpose flour
2/3 cup packed light brown sugar

Using your fingertips, combine the butter and flour in a small bowl, breaking the butter pieces into pea-size pieces. Mix in the brown sugar. The mixture will be crumbly.

IGUANAS

Green iguanas are vegetarians; they are the only reptiles who both live in and feed on trees. These lizards can grow to be six feet in length and weigh up to thirty pounds, and they look very much like miniature dinosaurs. These tropical iguanas are a bright, almost fluorescent, green. Ornamental spikes crest down their spines from their heads to their tails, and a dewlap (an extendable throat pouch) hangs beneath their chins. Males display their dewlaps to other iguanas to warn them off of occupied territory and to avoid real fighting.

Iguanas are fast runners, good climbers, and excellent swimmers and divers. Living in the trees along the riverbanks of tropical America, green iguanas spend their days basking in the sun and grazing on leaves. At the first hint of danger, they don't hesitate to throw themselves into the river. Diving to the bottom for protection, the lizards can stay submerged for several minutes until danger has passed. While they do prefer flight to fight, when cornered iguanas bite or strike out with their tails, using them as lashing whips. As an extreme measure, iguanas can shed their tails to escape capture; the tails will grow back, only without the decorative, serrated edges. When not sunning themselves or eating, iguanas retreat to their burrows in deep hollows along the riverbanks.

Iguanas are considered a delicacy in Mexico and Central America, where they have been eaten for thousands of years. Columbus reported seeing "a dragon about six-feet long which we killed with lances…the meat is white and tastes like chicken." A method of hunting iguanas involves a team effort. Young boys walk along the riverbank looking for their prey; when they spot an iguana, one boy will frighten it, scaring the iguana into the water to hide. The other boys, who are waiting along the riverbank, then jump in the river to capture it.

Iguanas hold a religious and spiritual significance for many forest peoples. To many Maya, the four aspects of the sky and earth were represented by the double-headed iguana dragon. A huge temple built to honor the giant iguana, *Itzam-Ye,* has been recently excavated in Honduras. Among the Cuña of Panama, the iguana is renown for its clever ways: According to myth he tricked *El Tigre* into giving fire to humankind.

Because iguanas are efficient converters of plant matter to protein, they have become the focus of a project by Dr. Dagmar Werner on an experimental farm in Costa Rica. Dr. Werner has proposed raising iguanas as a meat source in the tropics—a sort of "chicken of the trees." This would help save the rain forest since cattle ranching destroys the trees and soil and the delicate balance of the tropical ecosystem.

achiote paste   A mixture of ground achiote seeds, vinegar, garlic, and spices. Achiote paste is available in Latin food stores, sometimes called *recado colorado*. There is really no substitute for the smoky flavor of achiote, but if necessary, mix 2 tablespoons mild paprika with 2 teaspoons garlic powder, 1 teaspoon cumin, ½ teaspoon black pepper, ½ teaspoon salt, ¼ teaspoon cayenne pepper, and 2 tablespoons distilled white vinegar. This will give the color and some of the "zing" of achiote.

avocados   The dark, rough-skinned Haas avocados have a buttery, rich, creamy taste and texture. The larger, shiny avocados with the thin, light-green skins tend to be watery tasting with little flavor. Choose the Haas.

cactus pears   Fruit of the nopal cactus. These are seasonal. Available in supermarkets and Latin markets.

cajeta   Caramelized goat's milk and sugar sold in jars. A delicious specialty of central Mexico. Available in Latin markets. Sweetened condensed milk is an acceptable substitute.

Cajun spices/Cajun blackening spices   Used to coat seafood before pan searing or grilling. With heat, the spices become caramelized and turn black. If you can't find any in the supermarket spice section, mix your own—it's not difficult. See page 61.

cayenne pepper/ground red chile pepper   Not to be confused with chili powder, a mixture of chile and spices used to make chili beans. Cayenne pepper or red chile pepper is ground dried red chile peppers. Available in the spice section at supermarkets.

chipotle chiles (en adobo)   Chipotles are large, smoked, dried jalapeños sold canned in a spicy tomato sauce. Available in some supermarkets, in Latin food stores, and through mail order.

cilantro   Also known as Chinese parsley, cilantro is the fresh, green leaves of the coriander plant; the dried seeds are the spice called coriander. Fresh cilantro is available in many supermarkets as well as in Asian and Latin markets.

crème fraîche/crema Mexicana   Thick cultured milk used as a garnish on many Latin dishes. Make your own (see page 40), or find it sold under various names in Latin markets. If you must, you can substitute sour cream, but it's not the same!

habanero chiles   The hottest chile known, habaneros have a distinctive fruity fragrance and flavor. Available in Latin markets. If necessary, fresh jalapeños can be substituted, usually at a ratio of two jalapeños to one habanero.

Ibarra chocolate   There is really no substitute for the flavor of the Mexican-style chocolate. This chocolate is a mixture of cacao nibs—the heart of the cocoa bean—sugar, cinnamon, and almonds. Ibarra is the brand name of Mexican chocolate most commonly available in the United States. Ibarra chocolate comes in 3-ounce cakes that are sold in boxes of six. Mexican chocolate is available in some supermarkets and in Latin markets and it's available through mail order (page 153).

jerk seasoning/spices   Flavorful Jamaican spice mixture used for chicken, pork, and even seafood. If you can't find jerk in the spice section of the supermarket, mix your own. It isn't difficult to make—especially the dry mix. See page 62.

jícama   Plump tubers with dark brown skins and crisp, white flesh. They can be found in the produce section with potatoes and yams in many supermarkets as well as in Latin and Asian markets.

Key limes   Native to Florida, and almost impossible to find on the market, especially outside of that state. Substitute *fresh* lime juice from limes available in your supermarket.

lemon juice/lime juice   There is no substitute for the fresh lemon or lime juices called for in these recipes. Bottled lemon or lime preparations will not give desirable results.

masa harina   Specially ground cornmeal made from dried corn soaked in lime and used for making tortillas and tamales. Quaker makes a masa harina available in many supermarkets in the flour and sugar section; also in Latin markets and through mail order.

passionfruit/passionfruit glaze   A wonderfully fragrant fruit, which is very difficult to find on the market. Some companies are now making tropical juice combinations which include passionfruit along with orange and pineapple or peach juice. Passionfruit Glaze can be substituted for Apricot-Lime Glaze: Purée 2 tablespoons apricot jam, 2 tablespoons corn syrup, 1 teaspoon fresh lime juice, and 1 teaspoon cider vinegar. Makes approximately ⅓ cup.

plantains/platanos   Large cooking bananas, used as a starch in soups and stews and for frying when green, or baked as a dessert when sweet and ripe. Available in Latin and Asian markets.

quinoa   An Andean grain (pronounced *keen'-wah*) very high in protein. Available in natural food stores and through mail order.

Serrano chiles   Small tapered chiles with a snappy, fresh bite. If necessary, fresh jalapeños can be substituted one for one.

Seville oranges   The "bitter orange" used in Mayan marinades and cooking. The juices of ½ grapefruit, 1 orange, and 2 limes, mixed together, will produce a reasonable substitute.

tamarind   Sweet-sour pulp contained in the large pods of a tree native to Asia and North Africa. Extensively used as flavoring in East Indian and Middle Eastern cuisine, and popular in Caribbean cooking, tamarind paste can be found in Latin and Asian markets. Mango chutney, available in the condiment section of supermarkets, can be used as a substitute for tamarind paste. For tamarind glaze: purée 2 tablespoons mango chutney, 2 tablespoons corn syrup, and 2 teaspoons cider vinegar. Makes about ¼ cup.

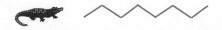 

MAIL ORDER

ail order can be fun. The prices are quite reasonable, and it will save you lots of time searching specialty food stores in your area. It will also open up a world of foods and flavors you may not otherwise experience. So, go ahead and order what you need. You won't be sorry.

El Cocodrilo/Chef's Pride
1996½ Sunset Drive
Pacific Grove, CA 93950
Phone or fax: 408-375-7108
e-mail: cocofish@cocofish.com

Mail-order items include jerk seasoning, Cajun blackening spices, habanero hot sauce, gumbo filé, Brazil nuts, achiote, masa harina, chipotle chiles, wild rice, quinoa, Mexican chocolate, and Japanese bread crumbs.

Mo Hotta—Mo Betta
465 Pacific Street
San Luis Obispo, CA 93401
800-462-3220

A great chile, salsa, and hot sauce catalog source.

Old Southwest Trading Company
P.O. Box 7545
Albuquerque, NM 87194
505-836-0168

Dried chiles, hot sauces, and Southwestern foods.

Melissa's World Variety Produce
P.O. Box 21127
Los Angeles, CA 90021
800-533 1870

Exotic produce, fresh habeneros, and other fresh and dried chiles. Mininum case purchase required on fresh fruits and vegetables.

Penderly's
1221 Manufacturing
Fort Worth, TX 75207
800-533-1870

Spices, condiments, and seasonings.

Dean & Deluca
560 Broadway
New York, NY 10012
800-221-7714

Wide variety of imported and specialty foods.

Los Chileros de Nuevo Mexico
P.O. Box 6215
Sante Fe, NM 87501
505-471-6967

Fresh and dried chiles, Southwestern food items.

El Cocodrilo/The Crocodile's Bodega
1996½ Sunset Drive
Pacific Grove, CA 93950
Phone or fax: 408-375-7108
e-mail: cocofish@cocofish.com

Available through The Crocodile's Bodega mail order:

Habanero Hot Sauce

Cajun Blackening Spices

Raspberry Melba Sauce

Achiote Paste

Wild Rice

Spices

Ibarra Mexican Chocolate

Gumbo Filé

Mango Chutney

Black Beans

Masa Harina

Jamaican Jerk Spices

Chipotle Chiles in Adobo

Brazil Nuts

Quinoa

Japanese Bread Crumbs

Phone, fax, e-mail, or mail coupon for free catalog.

Name: _____

Address:_____

City: _____ State: _____ Zip Code: _____

Phone: _____

Mail to: El Cocodrilo/The Crocodile's Bodega, 1996½ Sunset Drive, Pacific Grove, CA 93950

REFERENCES

F or those of you who wish to explore the rain forest and its denizens or the culinary, technical, or historical aspects of New World cuisine in greater depth, here are some places to begin.

Ackart, Robert C. *Fruits in Cooking: A Selection of Unusual and Classic Fruit Recipes.* New York: Macmillan, 1973.

Alper, Joseph. "Hot and Healthy." *Self* (Jan. 1992), 86–89.

Animals in Your Zoo. Portland, OR: Metro Washington Park Zoo, 1990.

Ayersu, Edward S., ed. *Jungles.* Washington, DC: Smithsonian Institution, 1980.

Batterbury, Michael, and Ariane Batterbury. "Columbus Makes Waves." *Food Arts* (Oct. 1991), 28–35.

Behler, John L. "That's a Croc." *Wildlife Conservation* (Sept.–Oct. 1993), 70–71.

Brown, Dale M., ed. *Aztecs: Reign of Blood and Splendor.* Alexandria, VA: Time-Life Books, 1992.

Brown, Dale M., ed. *Incas: Lords of Gods and Glory.* Alexandria, VA: Time-Life Books, 1968.

Brown, Dale M., ed. *The Magnificent Maya.* Alexandria, VA: Time-Life Books, 1993.

Carcione, Joe, and Bob Lucas. *The Green Grocer.* San Francisco: Chronicle Books, 1972.

Caufield, Catherine. *In the Rainforest.* Chicago: University of Chicago Press, 1984.

Crosby, Alfred W., Jr. *The Colombian Exchange.* Westport, CT: Greenwood Press, 1972.

Crump, Donald J., ed. *National Geographic Book of Mammals,* vols. 1–2. Washington, DC: National Geographic Society, 1981.

De Beer, Sir Gavin, et al., eds. *Encyclopedia of the Animal World,* 21 vols. Lausanne, Switzerland: Elsevier International Projects Ltd., 1972.

Fisher, Ron et al. *Emerald Realm: Earth's Precious Rainforests.* Washington, D.C.: National Geographic Society, 1990.

Forsyth, Adrian, and Ken Miyata. *Tropical Nature*. New York: Charles Scribner's Sons, 1984.

Gray, Ralph, ed. *Secrets of Animal Survival. Books for Young Explorers*. Washington, DC: National Geographic Society, 1983.

Hale, William Harlan. *Horizon Cookbook and Illustrated History of Eating and Drinking Through the Ages*. New York: American Heritage, 1968.

Herbst, Sharon Tyler. *The Food Lover's Companion*. Hauppauge, NY: Barron's Educational Series, Inc., 1990.

Hunt, Joni Phelps. *A Chorus of Frogs*. San Luis Obispo, CA: Blake Publishing, 1992.

Hyatt, Derril A. *Foods America Gave the World*. Boston: L.C. Page and Co., 1937.

Jennings, Gary. *Aztec*. New York: Avon Books, 1980.

Johnson, William Weber. *The Andean Republics*. New York: Time-Life Books, 1965.

Larousse Encyclopedia of Animal Life. London: Hamlyn, 1972.

Leonard, Jonathan Norton. *The First Farmers*. Alexandria, VA: Time-Life Books, 1973.

Leonard, Jonathan Norton. *Latin American Cooking*. Alexandria, VA: Time-Life Books, 1968.

Michener, James A. *Caribbean*. New York: Ballantine Books, 1989.

National Fish and Seafood Promotional Council. *Fish and Seafood Made Easy*. U.S. Department of Commerce, Washington, D.C., 1989.

Olaya, Clara Ines. "Caju/Marañon/Merey/Acaiu/Cashew Nut." *Americas* 42, no. 3 (1990), 52–53.

Popescu, Petru. *Amazon Beaming*. New York: Viking, 1991.

Quintana, Patricia. *Feasts of Life*. Tulsa, OK: Council Oak Books, 1989.

Rhoades, Robert E. "Corn, the Golden Grain." *National Geographic* (June 1993), 93–117.

Robertiello, Jack. "Desert Fruits Prick Appetites." *Americas* 47, no. 4 (1995), 58–59.

Robertiello, Jack. "Peanut/Maní /Cacahuete." *Americas* 43, no. 4 (1991), 58–59.

Robertiello, Jack. "Piña/Ananas/Pineapple/Abacaxi." *Americas* 42, no. 4 (1990), 54–55.

Robertiello, Jack. "Xitomatle/Tomato/Tomate/Jítomate." *Americas* 42 no. 5 (1990), 54–55.

Ross, Charles A., ed. *Crocodiles and Alligators*. New York: Facts on File, 1989.

Schneider, Elizabeth. "Spotlight on Tropical Tubers and Other Starchy Staples." *Food Arts* (Jan.–Feb. 1992).

Schneider, Elizabeth. *Uncommon Fruits and Vegetables, a Commonsense Guide*. New York: Harper & Row, 1986.

Schweid, Richard. *Hot Peppers.* New Orleans: New Orleans School of Cooking, 1987.

Sokolov, Raymond. *Why We Eat What We Eat.* New York: Summit Books, 1991.

Swartz, John. "The Great Food Migration." *Newsweek* 118 (Special issue: Fall/Winter 1991), 58–62.

Tannahill, Reay. *Food in History.* New York: Stein & Day, 1973.

Thorbjarnarson, John. "Crocodile Lakes of Hispanola." *Wildlife Conservation* (Jan.–Feb. 1990), 42–47.

Viola, Herman J., and Carolyn Margolis. *Seeds of Change.* Washington, DC: Smithsonian Institution Press, 1991.

Von Welanetz, Diana, and Paul Von Welanetz. *Guide to Ethnic Ingredients.* Los Angeles: J. P. Tarcher, 1982.

Wexo, John Bonnett. *Zoobooks: Alligators and Crocodiles.* San Diego: Wildlife Education, Ltd., Dec. 1990.

Wexo, John Bonnett. *Zoobooks: Endangered Animals.* San Diego: Wildlife Education, Ltd., Jan. 1984.

Wilson, Edward O. "Rainforest Canopy, the High Frontier." *National Geographic* (Dec. 1991), 78–106.

 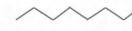

INDEX